A. C. FRIZZELL
His Life and Times

Florida Land Baron
Charlotte County Legend

A Biography
by
Cheryl Frizzell

cherylfrizzell@yahoo.com

Designed by Cheryl Frizzell

Printed in the United States of America.

Unless otherwise noted,
all photographs, maps, illustrations, and other images
are either the property of or created by Cheryl Frizzell.

Custom cover designed by Cheryl Frizzell; created by Cover Creator.
1948 Cover Photograph of A. C. Frizzell, age 58.

ACKNOWLEDGMENTS

Many thanks to my brother Steve, our family genealogist, who has diligently and intelligently worked his way through the annals of time and made many outstanding and meaningful discoveries and contributions. He was there for me every step of the way in writing this book. His analytical thoughtfulness was very helpful, as was his ever present enthusiasm and support.

Excerpts from the Daniel Child diaries are courtesy of the Charlotte County Historical Center, gift of Vernon and Edna Jane Peeples. Various photographs of early Murdock are also courtesy of the Charlotte County Historical Center.

The Charlotte County Historical Center
514 East Grace Street
Punta Gorda, FL 33950
941/629-7278
Charlotte County, Florida, History Collections Online
http://ccflhistory.contentdm.oclc.org/cdm/

Many thanks to Annette Snapp, Historian (Community Services), Charlotte County Historical Center, for her diligent assistance and inspiring enthusiasm.

Legal transactions are abstracted from more than 500 recorded documents found in the records of Charlotte County and various surrounding counties.

NOTE TO THE READER

For a simple point of reference, add a zero to dollar amounts in this book for approximate 2018 values.

CONTENTS

He was one of those self-made men
who climbed outside his skin
from a childhood behind a plow
and schoolin' enough to know how.

"Education is fine," he declared more than once,
"but you've got to have something else."
This is the story of *something else*.

INTRODUCTION

A small rustic sign stood in front of Granddaddy's small white frame house on Highway 41 in Murdock, where Frizzell Lane and the Charlotte County Administration are located today. The sign identified the headquarters of one of Florida's largest cattle ranches, AP CATTLE RANCH, named for Daddy (Arthur Paul Frizzell) and owned by Granddaddy (Arthur Cleveland Frizzell).

Cradled between two wood fence posts, the unobtrusive sign spoke softly of the grandness of Granddaddy's empire at the peak of his power in 1947, the year of the below photograph. It whispered no hint of *something else*.

Highway 41 in the background.

By 1947, Granddaddy had become a living legend in Southwest Florida. Over the previous thirty years, he had shrewdly advanced and diversified his career interests from railroad clerk to turpentine and timber tycoon, cattle baron, and business entrepreneur. During that time, he acquired more than 100,000 acres in Charlotte and surrounding counties, while leasing another 100,000, and he built himself an empire on the land that would later become the city of Port Charlotte.

In 1954 when he sold 78,000 acres of his land to Port Charlotte's developers, it was the largest private land transaction in the history of Florida.

THE PROMISED LAND

When you see the children
dancing in the December sunshine,
with yellow oranges in their hands,
you realize that this is indeed the 'Promised Land.'

Little is known about Granddaddy's family prior to the 1800s. It is probable that his ancestors migrated from Scotland, possibly as early as 1609, with a stop in Ireland for an indeterminate amount of time, before continuing onward across the Atlantic Ocean to eventually settle in the Carolinas.

By the early 1800s, they were living in Spartanburg County, South Carolina, but their migration did not stop there. In about 1847, they moved through western South Carolina and across Georgia to a place in Alabama called Davis Gap, located fifteen miles southeast of Gadsden. In Davis Gap, they bought 40- and 80-acre tracts of Alabama public land dirt cheap through a special government grant in exchange for a commitment to homestead.

A couple of generations later, Granddaddy's parents lived on one of those tracts of land in a small frame house, where he was born on June 19, 1890. He was the second born of eight children, seven of whom would live to adulthood.

The Frizzell family and Alabama home, Granddaddy on the far right, c. 1903.

By the time that Granddaddy was ten years old, he was working as a "farm laborer," according to the 1900 U. S. Federal Census. He did not attend school, but could read and write. He had quit school at an early age to work on the family farm to help feed his large family. Although later described as the proverbial self-made man with an eighth grade education, he only completed the first five grades of school.

The census also reveals that Granddaddy's father could not read or write, and it lists three boarders living with the family in the little farm house pictured above. They worked at a nearby sawmill. Perhaps they talked about the sawmill or took young Granddaddy to work with them. In any case, sawmills would later play a major role in his great success.

Ten years later, in the 1910 census when Granddaddy was twenty years old, he had left the farm and was living in Gadsden, where he boarded in a house with a 55-year-old widow and her family. He worked as a millwright in a steel plant there, but he studied bookkeeping in his spare time.

Then on March 13, 1913, in Waycross, Georgia, he married Martha Elizabeth "Miss Pattie" Bloodworth (Standifer), who was twenty years his elder. Why they married in Waycross, 350 miles from Gadsden, is a mystery. There is no known evidence that links either one of them to Waycross, but their marriage is clearly recorded in the Ware County official records.

At the time of their marriage, Granny had been the widow of a prominent Gadsden railroad man for about two years, and she was working as manager of the Postal Telegraph and Cable Company. She was originally from Oak Bowery, Alabama, and she had two children: Annabel, age 12, and Lemuel, age 16 (only six years younger than his new stepfather).

Family lore says that Granny was Granddaddy's Sunday school teacher, and that is how they met, but in a 1948 newspaper interview, Granny said, "I met him up in Rock Springs, Alabama [one mile from the Frizzell home]. He came around one Sunday afternoon, while the Sunday school class I taught was preparing to go for a walk. I told some of the girls to ask him if he would like to go on the walk, but they were too bashful to ask him; so, I asked him, and he accepted. I was older than he was, and I have always said that I took advantage of his youth; and he is always saying, 'When are you going to grow up?'"[1]

Granddaddy in 1913.

After Granddaddy and Granny married, they lived in a duplex house in Gadsden with Granny's two children, and they all four worked. The 1914 City Directory indicates that Granny continued working as manager of the postal telegraph office, while 17-year-old Lemuel worked as an electrician, and 13-year-old Annabel was a telephone operator for Southern Bell Telephone and Telegraph Company. Granddaddy had left the steel plant and was working as a shipping clerk for the Tennessee, Alabama, and Georgia Railway, a small railroad with only 92 miles of track that had been created in

1890 to haul coal from Lookout Mountain. The track started in Chattanooga, ran the length of the mountain, and ended in Gadsden.

Granddaddy's older brother, Lon Forney, lived with his wife, Lucy, and their one-year-old daughter, Kathryn, in the other half of the duplex. Uncle Forney worked as a hostler for the same railroad where Granddaddy worked. A hostler serviced the engines at the end of the runs.

A year later, Granddaddy, Granny, and Annabel were living in a small South Florida town called Ona, located about fifty miles inland from Sarasota. The Report of the Secretary of State for 1915-1916 lists Granny as a Notary Public there and Granddaddy as a Justice of the Peace.

Lemuel, who had planned to attend college in Alabama, did not move to Ona with his family. In 1916, he attended Alabama Polytechnic Institute, State College for the Benefit of Agricultural and the Mechanic Arts (now Auburn University).

The family's move to Florida is another early mystery, perhaps attributable to the "pioneer spirit." Granddaddy and Granny had left their family and friends in Alabama and migrated 600 miles south from Gadsden, where they both had good jobs, to a Podunk town in the middle of nowhere in the wild state of Florida for one railroad job between the two of them. Granny had taught Granddaddy how to operate the telegraph, and the two of them worked one station agent job for the Charlotte Harbor and Northern Railway (C. H. & N.).

The C. H. & N. was a subsidiary of the American Agricultural Chemical Company, and its main purpose was the transportation of phosphate. Its tracks led about 100 miles from a town called Mulberry in Central Florida, to a 3,000-foot-long dock at Boca Grande on Gasparilla Island in the Gulf of Mexico. There, phosphate was loaded directly from railroad cars to large ships for delivery to ports all over the world.

Commonly used acronyms for C. H. & N. suggest that the railroad fell short in matters unrelated to phosphate. Its passengers called it the "Crackers, Hobos, and Niggers" railroad, while its employees called it the "Cold, Hungry, and Naked" railroad, because they thought their manager was a stingy money-grubber, who cut too many costs in an effort to stretch the dollar.

Phosphate docks at Boca Grande. 19--.
Black & white photonegative, 4 x 5 in. State Archives of Florida, Florida Memory.
<https://www.floridamemory.com/items/show/294723>, (accessed 5 April 2019).

A wooden cleat,
the last vestige of Port Boca Grande phosphate dock
on display at the Boca Grande Lighthouse, 2015.

C. H. & N. Train and Boca Grande Passenger Depot 1926
The Burgett Brothers.
"Courtesy, Tampa-Hillsborough County Public Library System."
http://digitalcollections.hcplc.org/digital/collection/p15391coll1/id/2588/rec/19, (accessed April 26, 2018).

Boca Grande Passenger Depot in 2015, now shops and a restaurant.

More than a year after moving to Ona, on May 8, 1916, Granddaddy and Granny bought a house beside the railroad track there for $325. The house would have been on the left where the building is in the background of the below 2015 photo of downtown Ona.

In the forefront of the above gas station/convenience store, there are several blocks with small houses and an old Baptist church that Granddaddy and Granny would have attended when they lived there. The church was established in 1914, the year before they arrived.

On January 8, 1917, Granddaddy registered for the draft for World War I. He was "tall" with a "stout" build, "blue" eyes, and "black" hair. He lived in Ona, and he worked as agent and operator for the Charlotte Harbor and Northern Railway Company in Vandolah, Florida. At some point in the past two years, he had transferred two miles up the road, due north, from a railroad station at Ona to one at Vandolah.

At the time, Vandolah was a busy little town with a hotel, general store, post office, school, and a sawmill. In 1917 and in 1920, the Wauchula Development Company was there operating "a 16-mile logging railroad with a mill of 25,000-foot capacity."[2]

Now, all that remains of Vandolah is a railroad crossing, and it is listed among Florida's many ghost towns.

Vandolah in 2015.

While Granddaddy was working in Vandolah, Granny started working ten miles to the east as manager of the Western Union office in Wauchula during the area's greatest truck farm season. "She handled the volume of business in a manner that won the praise of all."[3]

After Granny had worked for six months at Western Union, she and Granddaddy moved with Annabel to another small town on the railroad called Murdock, about forty-five miles southwest of Ona, but still in the huge, sparsely-populated county of DeSoto, that would later be divided into five counties. Murdock was strategically located about twenty miles inland from Boca Grande at the intersection of the future Highways 41 and 776.

From the time that Granddaddy and Granny were married in Waycross in 1913, they had lived in Gadsden for two years and in Ona for three years. Now, they would live in Murdock, where they would permanently settle and build an empire.

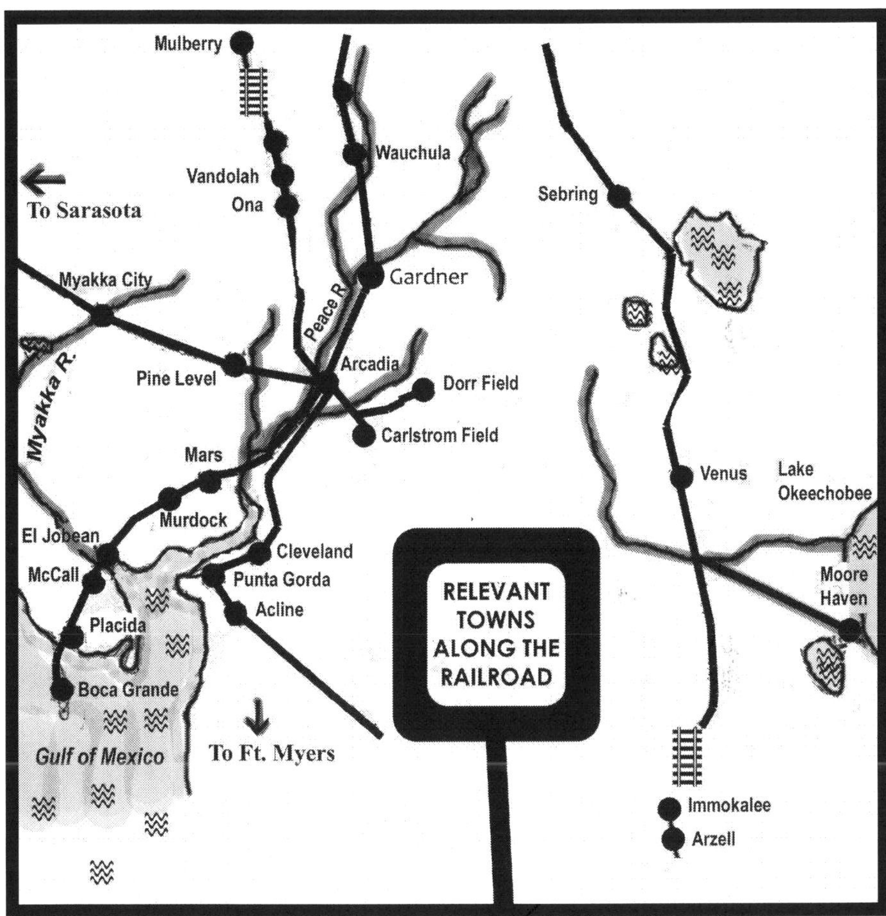

Murdock, originally called Charlotte, had been established by the C. H. & N. in 1907. Its name derived from Charlotte Harbor, which the English had named in 1775 in tribute to their Queen Charlotte, wife of King George III. Charlotte had first served only as a fueling station for the wood-burning locomotives of the railway. Then in 1908, a depot and a post office opened there.

A couple of years later in 1910, along came a man named John M. Murdock, one of Florida's first real estate schemers. He bought 18,000 acres of land in the area, founded the Chicago-based Murdock Colony Farms, and began developing ten-acre tracts for truck farming. His first move was to give C. H. & N. some land along its right-of-way, and so the railroad changed the name of the place from Charlotte to Murdock. Then, he printed brochures advertising tracts of land for sale, and he guaranteed $1,000, if the land was not as represented.

The story of early Murdock unfolded in a series of articles in the *The Tampa Tribune* starting August 7, 1912, when it first mentioned Murdock. It reported that the post office there had been temporarily discontinued for undisclosed reasons.

A few months later, drainage operations began when civil engineers made a preliminary survey of an 18,000-acre tract of land for the Murdock Land Company. The engineers determined that the land averaged about seventeen feet above sea level, was some of the best in the area, and could be successfully drained.

By the beginning of 1913, many northern tourists and investors were discovering Murdock. They were visiting the area and purchasing large tracts of land there. They were "delighted" with the climate and with DeSoto County. They planned to improve their lands and to start truck farming on a large scale.

By the end of 1913, steam shovels were digging canals, and the county commissioners were pleased with the progress being made. It was one of the largest drainage plans ever undertaken in the county.

In the spring of 1914, John Murdock platted that part of Murdock located on the south side of the intersection of the future Highways 41 and 776 (now the Port Charlotte Town Center). He platted it into sixteen blocks, each containing twenty-four lots, for a total of 324 homesites. The lots averaged twenty-five feet wide by one hundred and thirty feet long.

During the next year, many people moved to Murdock. They built nice homes on the platted lots, and they started truck farming on the ten-acre tracts. They created a small bustling community with an active social life, and they prospered. Life was good, and they were filled with optimism.

Steamshovel Digging Canal at Murdock, Florida
Charlotte Harbor Area Historical Society and U.S. Cleveland
http://ccflhistory.contentdm.oclc.org/cdm/ref/collection/p15007coll1/id/429, (accessed April 26, 2018).

John Murdock, the developer and "well known capitalist of Murdock," was among those who settled there. He built himself and his family a mansion. Then, he went to Arcadia and purchased so many large orange trees for his home that it took eight freight cars to transport them.

On December 12, 1915, Mrs. G. L. Beall, a resident of Murdock from Butte, Montana, and wife of the local agent for the C. H. & N., wrote an article for *The Tampa Tribune*. In it, she praised Murdock, both the man and the town. The article (with no photos) appeared in the Sunday newspaper and was certainly good publicity.

> J. M. Murdock, of Chicago, has the distinction of having been the founder of the town and colony of Murdock... The entire area is a grass covered meadow similar in appearance to the plains of the West. This tract contains within its boundaries all the proven lands of Florida, including the muck of the lowlands, the black hammock, and the sandy loam of the uplands. The soil is, generally speaking, a dark sandy loam, with a yellow clay or lime shell subsoil (Florida's

guarantee of fertility), which is especially adapted to the growth of grapefruit, oranges and citrus fruit generally.

Our transportation connects with all railroads that reach Florida, as well as with all ocean-going steamers. At Boca Grande we have the deepest and best harbor on the Western coast of Florida, with gigantic steamers direct to New York. Our freight rates are about one-third those of California, with the principal markets of the United States much closer, and so the people of Murdock have the choice of either rail or water routes to Northern and Eastern markets.

The town of Murdock is surrounded by the colony lands, which are situated twenty-five miles southwest of Arcadia on the Charlotte Harbor & Northern Railroad.

The depot at Murdock is the finest of all the stations between Arcadia and Boca Grande with spacious living rooms upstairs.

Murdock Train Station, c.1915
Charlotte Harbor Area Historical Society and U.S. Cleveland http://ccflhistory.contentdm.oclc.org/cdm/ref/collection/p15007coll1/id/828, (accessed April 26, 2018).

We have a post office run by a postmistress, and a general merchandise store, which is run by Mr. Mearl R. Murdock, son of John Murdock.

First Post Office at Murdock, Florida and Postmaster, J. B. Moody, c.1908
Charlotte Harbor Area Historical Society and U.S. Cleveland, http://ccflhistory.contentdm.oclc.org/cdm/ref/collection/p15007coll1/id/8069, (accessed April 26, 2018).

Murdock Store, c.1912
Charlotte Harbor Area Historical Society and U.S. Cleveland http://ccflhistory.contentdm.oclc.org/cdm/ref/collection/p15007coll1/id/640, (accessed April 26, 2018).

The Murdock Colony Farms Company has its headquarters here. A secretary, who is also a notary public, works there.

Murdock Farms Colony Headquarters [the boarding house], c.1915
Charlotte Harbor Area Historical Society and U.S. Cleveland
http://ccflhistory.contentdm.oclc.org/cdm/ref/collection/p15007coll1/id/426, (accessed April 26, 2018).

A comfortable country hotel here serves as the meeting place for the Literary and Debating Club. The meetings are held every Wednesday evening. Everyone belongs to this club, and they all have a good time.

> Whenever a town has people who are contented with the present and have faith in the future and have the business ability to advance themselves and others, there you see the makings of a good town.

Mr. and Mrs. A. S. Christie from Seattle, Washington, are shipping farm products every day from their farm east of town. Their little daughter, Aneta, has the honor of being the first child born in the new town of Murdock.

Christy Bungalow at Murdock Farms Colony in Murdock, Florida, c.1915
Charlotte Harbor Area Historical Society and U.S. Cleveland
http://ccflhistory.contentdm.oclc.org/cdm/ref/collection/p15007coll1/id/428, (accessed April 26, 2018).

D. W. Child & Son, who are numbered among the most substantial citizens of this place, have a pony farm, where they raise Southern ponies. The Childs came here from Cuba where they still have large holdings of some of the best in Cuba. Mr. Child, Jr., is a deep student and also a practical farmer and can tell you a great deal about the farming business.

Daniel Child, Jr., was a man with an exceptional intellect and many talents. He was fluent in English, Spanish, and French. He was pianist and clerk for the Murdock Baptist Church. He kept church records that still exist for most years from 1922 through 1955. He also wrote diaries, twenty-nine of which still exist. The first was written in 1912 about his incredible journey with his father from Cuba to Key West, through Florida, and eventually to Murdock. His other diaries detail everyday life in Murdock from 1922 through 1955 and will be referenced throughout this book.

The most striking and important thing about this town is that it has the most complete system of drainage in the State of Florida. Without drainage – energy, faith and fertilizer is wasted. Our Southern paper asks: 'What is drainage?' and the answer they give is 'When a hole three feet deep is filled with water which disappears in twenty-four hours, then your land has drainage.'

Three immense land dredges have been at work here for the past sixteen months. In that time they have made forty-two miles of canal which practically cuts this land into three parts. These canals are cut down to rock and are fifteen feet wide at the bottom and forty feet wide at the top. They still have many miles of canals yet to cut and the payroll for this dredging concern for the month of November was $1,780.

When you sell land, you don't sell water. John Murdock has made good.

Now that the drainage question is settled here, what about the irrigation? Artesian wells are numerous at this place. There is one well ninety feet deep that throws eighty gallons of water per minute.

One of the current magazines asked last month, 'What is poverty?' The answer given was, 'Poverty is the lack of resources.' If this is so, then we do not have poverty here. With all these advantages, Murdock can rival the vinelands of Southern France, the olive groves of Italy, and the wheat fields of Walla Walla, Washington.

When you see the children dancing in the December sunshine, with yellow oranges in their hands, you realize that this is indeed the 'Promised Land.'

The following month toward the end of January 1916, John Murdock's wife, Ardesta, hosted a special affair of the season with a reception at her home for the Women's Guild of the Episcopal Church of Arcadia. A special coach was attached to the morning train from Arcadia for the conveyance of the guests, who were taken to her beautiful residence, where everything for their comfort and entertainment was provided. Fifty-eight guests sat at dinner at one time. After dinner, the party enjoyed an automobile ride over the Murdock estate.

The John Murdock Family Home, c.1915
Edith King on Porch of Murdock Home
Charlotte Harbor Area Historical Society and U.S. Cleveland
http://ccflhistory.contentdm.oclc.org/cdm/ref/collection/p15007coll1/id/427, (accessed April 26, 2018).

About three months later, the first in a series of events occurred that would send the settlement of Murdock on a downward spiral and lead to the loss of farms and homes there. A robbery at the general merchandise store, which was run by John Murdock's son, may or may not have been orchestrated, but it at least set the stage for what was yet to come.

On April 4, a large quantity and variety of merchandise was stolen from the store. The unknown person(s) stole $20 from the cash register, several pairs of good underwear and work clothes, expensive groceries, candy, and cigars. The intruder(s) then made a quiet getaway and left the back door ajar.

Twelve days later, John Murdock's wife and little daughter, Mordeste, left for Jacksonville, never to return.

Then that summer in July, John Murdock and his son Mearl filed for bankruptcy. Creditors simultaneously filed a petition asking to be paid in the amount of $26.23 to a plumbing supply company and a total of $666.82 to two different hardware companies.

In August, only eight months after Mrs. Beall's laudatory newspaper article, John Murdock sold the entire Murdock tract in order to satisfy a mortgage on it. The sale included the land that he had sold to the many happy Murdock folks. He had given them deeds without clear title, and the deeds were worthless. By then, some of the best farms in the state were on that tract, almost all of them under cultivation, and fine dwellings had been built.

John Murdock's next appearance was in Tampa during the spring of 1917. He was staying in one of Tampa's plush hotels, as usual, while tending to business matters there and shaking hands with all of his Tampa friends, who respected him as a prominent Floridian and welcomed him with open arms.

Then on April 14, he sent a telegram from Washington, D. C., to a member of the Tampa Board of Trade.

> Have you any shipyard or deep water frontage that would be immediately available for construction of large wooden boats to be built of Florida pine? Kindly advise me by wire here. We have just been awarded contract by government for several boats.

The week before, the U. S. had joined its allies Britain, France, and Russia to fight in World War I. Prior to that, Germany had already destroyed several U. S. ships.

John Murdock did not find what he needed to build ships in Tampa, but he did find it in Jacksonville, and so he moved there, and he proceeded with his new plan.

That summer, he was indicted in Federal Court in Jacksonville on a charge of using the mails to defraud in connection with the sale of more than $250,000 worth of land in and adjacent to Murdock. He was only able to make good a few of his sales, but he was clever enough to transfer the others to another tract of land east of Arcadia, where he did the same thing. He managed to avoid recording the mortgage he had on that property, too, and so *twice*, he sold what he did not possess and could not afford to possess.

Only seven Murdock deeds were found with holders who could prosecute. All of the others were barred by the statute of limitations. Apparently, he settled with the seven, and the case was dropped.

Earlier in 1917, the Murdock general store had gone bankrupt, and Murdock's wife had sued him for divorce and won.

John Murdock had left behind a trail of broken dreams, while he continued to live the high life, then in Jacksonville, and to build ships for the U. S. government. He contracted to build eight freighters, but he only built three, the last one being the *St. George*, delivered in 1919.

> June 25, 1918, **JAX LAUNCHES FIRST SHIP**
> [In Jacksonville] The *Dancey*, the first wooden hull steamer to be built here under government contract, was launched from the ways of the J. M Murdock Shipbuilding Company ... Within ten minutes after the *Dancey* was launched the keel of another vessel was laid.
>
> September 3, 1918
> **GOVERNOR AT JACKSONVILLE CELEBRATION**
> [In Jacksonville] One ship was launched here today in connection with the Labor day celebration, the steamer *Mariah*, built by the J. M. Murdock Shipbuilding Company ...

About the same time that John Murdock started building his first ship in Jacksonville, Granddaddy, Granny, and Annabel arrived in Murdock, then with a population of 145 and still very much in the wilderness of untamed Florida. It was accessible only by train or by horse and buggy on two-rut dirt trails.

The closest shopping was eight miles to the south in the seaport community of Punta Gorda, with a population of about 1,000 at the time. A two-rut, dirt wagon track led from Murdock through the palmettos and pines to a ferry that traveled a mile across the Peace River from Charlotte Harbor (Town) to Punta Gorda. By 1916, construction of a bridge had begun there, but World War I had interfered with its completion.

Marian Avenue from King Street - Punta Gorda, Florida. ca 1910.
Black & white photonegative, 4 x 5 in. State Archives of Florida, Florida Memory.
<https://www.floridamemory.com/items/show/153110>, (accessed 26 April 2018).

When the Frizzells first stepped off the train in Murdock, they stood on the platform of the two-story train depot, where they would live in the "spacious" quarters upstairs.

From the platform, they saw the silent buildings of a once bustling community, all buildings that they would eventually own. Across the dirt ruts of the future Highway 776, looking from west to east, they saw a sleepy post office, with only a postmaster and an occasional patron to keep it awake. They saw an abandoned general store and a two-story boarding house that had once served as headquarters for the Murdock Colony Farms. Next to the boarding house and located so that it could easily be seen from the dirt ruts of the future Highway

41, they saw the Murdock Hotel, that had once hosted social gatherings, such as weekly Literary and Debating Club meetings.

The Frizzells climbed the stairs to their new home in the depot, where they all three would live, but only Granddaddy would work there. While "the popular agent of the C. H. & N." conveniently worked downstairs, Annabel attended high school in Arcadia, and Granny worked as station agent in a little railroad town called Gardner, located forty miles from Murdock and ten miles north of Arcadia.

Passengers Waiting at the Charlotte Harbor and Northern Railroad Station in Murdock

Charlotte Harbor Area Historical Society and U.S. Cleveland http://ccflhistory.contentdm.oclc.org/cdm/ref/collection/p15007coll1/id/3958, (accessed April 26, 2018).

Granddaddy and Granny held similar, if not identical positions, but Granddaddy earned $68 per month, while Granny earned $50 per month, perhaps a case of wage inequality. Considering that Granny had taught Granddaddy the business, and she had managed the postal telegraph office in Gadsden and the Western Union office in Wauchula, a possible explanation for her lower salary would be her gender. Her right to vote would not happen for two years, but her right to equal pay would not happen in her entire lifetime.

Although their two salaries totaled only $118 per month, Granddaddy thought it was a lot of money in the land of plenty, where he and his family easily lived off the land. He worked a vegetable farm behind the depot, and he hunted in the bountiful Murdock woods.

He hunted turkey, deer, and quail, and he hunted wild boar and scrub cattle that had both been running wild since the Spaniards dumped them there 400 years before in the 1500s. The cattle were as vicious as the boars and as likely to turn on a man and attack. Their beef was tough and stringy, too, perhaps the reason that Granddaddy's favorite part of a steak was the fat. Folks used to joke that after they cooked the tough meat, they threw it away and cut the gravy with a knife.

Granny gathered eggs (Granny's Photo Album).

During their first summer in Murdock, while Granny was working forty miles away in Gardner and making occasional business trips to Tampa and to Lakeland, she somehow found the time to establish herself as a leader in the community and as a woman who made things happen.

Her first project was a war savings stamps rally in June 1918. She advertised in the newspaper that Murdock, although a very small place, would have a war savings stamps rally, "just the same as other larger towns and cities." Much interest was being shown, and the residents hoped for a big day and the sale of many stamps.

Then in September, she served as Murdock's chairperson for the Women's Fourth Liberty Loan effort to raise funds for the U. S. military.

Also in that first summer, Granny's son Lemuel (L. B. Standifer in the below photo) arrived in Murdock, and he worked at Dorr Field, which was one of two airfields near Arcadia, then known as "Aviation City." The airfields were used for military flight training operations during both world wars. Florida was selected for the operations, because its weather ranked second best for flyable days, with Arizona having slightly more and Texas ranking third.

Dorr Field was probably the home base for seven airplanes that flew over Murdock one day that summer, furnishing its residents with a "chief amusement of watching the sky for birdmen." Some had never seen an airplane before.

On the weekends when Lemuel was not working, he joined his sister Annabel and other young people of Murdock to travel three miles for casual afternoons spent bathing in the health-giving water at Salt Springs. In the evenings back in Murdock, they enjoyed chaperoned dinners, usually either at the Frizzell or the Daniel Child residence.

Then in August, Lemuel was inducted into the service at Arcadia, with World War I ending only two and a half months later, on November 11 (Veterans Day). From Arcadia, he went to a couple of training camps in the U. S. and was discharged in January. He then returned to college in Alabama.

Shortly after Lemuel left, Annabel started teaching school in Murdock. She had graduated in June with a class of thirty-two from DeSoto High School in Arcadia.

> July 18, 1918, **LOST**
> STRAYED – From station at Murdock, Fla., one light-cream-colored Jersey cow, slightly swaybacked, tips of horns sawed off about an inch and half. One white and yellow heifer calf, nine months old, wearing a muzzle weaner. Liberal reward for return to me, or information leading to recovery.
> A. C. Frizzell, Murdock, Fla.

> September 29, 1918, **FOR EXCHANGE**
> WILL EXCHANGE – Pair mules, well matched, and wagon and harness for Ford, wide tread, 1916, 1917 or 1918 model.
> Address Box 55, Murdock, Fla. [the Frizzell address]

Fall that year brought heavy rains that flooded the Murdock truck farms and discouraged planting for that season, although Granddaddy's chufas survived, and he put a lot of fine hogs on them. Turns out, they were the best chufas raised in the area, and they showed what could be done by the right kind of farming. He had raised them on the old Schlosstine place, which was one of the abandoned farms left behind in the wake of John Murdock's fraudulent scheme.

After the floods, came an influenza epidemic that closed school and sent Granddaddy to visit his sick father in Alabama. By the time he returned, Granny had organized a Sunday School at Murdock, and she was serving as secretary and treasurer. Then, Granddaddy's brother Lon Forney and his little daughter, Katheryn (age 5), arrived for a visit, and they stayed for several weeks.

While they were visiting, a crew of Murdock men went to Boca Grande to assist in loading a ship with phosphate. Since the war had ended the month before, phosphate trains had passed through Murdock daily.

The phosphate trains would continue operating there until 1979, when the Boca Grande port closed, no longer able to compete with Tampa's growing port.

My brother Steve remembers the trains passing through the nearby town of El Jobean in the early 1960s. Each train could have as many as five locomotives and over 100 phosphate cars. When a train passed at night, a thrill for everyone was to turn the porch lights on and off, signaling for the engineer to blow the horn.

Steve said that fishermen on the railroad bridge over the Myakka River would climb down on the trestle beneath, while the train crossed on the track above them. The fishermen used cane poles with wire, instead of line, and they used slabs of bacon for bait to catch red fish and snook that weighed twenty-five and thirty pounds.

TURPENTINE AND TIMBER

“We just naturally wanted land that adjoined ours.”

And so it was that for two years, Granddaddy and Granny lived in Murdock and saved their money. They lived upstairs in the train depot, while they worked for the railroad, earning $118 per month, most of which they saved. Granddaddy added to their savings by joining his neighbors in truck farming and raising hogs, along with some cattle, on the abandoned Schlosstine place.

Then on January 1, 1920, Granddaddy took a giant step forward and spent $800 for a four-year turpentine lease on about 760 acres of land on the south and north sides of the platted town of Murdock. In the lease, the owners of the pine land reserved the right to fence, pasture, and/or cultivate it, but without in any way interfering with Granddaddy's entry, occupation, and use of the land for the purpose of boxing and working the timber for turpentine.

The shaded yellow area on the below section map indicates the land included in Granddaddy's turpentine lease; the small aqua rectangle inside the shaded yellow area indicates the platted town of Murdock. Each numbered square is a section that measures one mile by one mile.

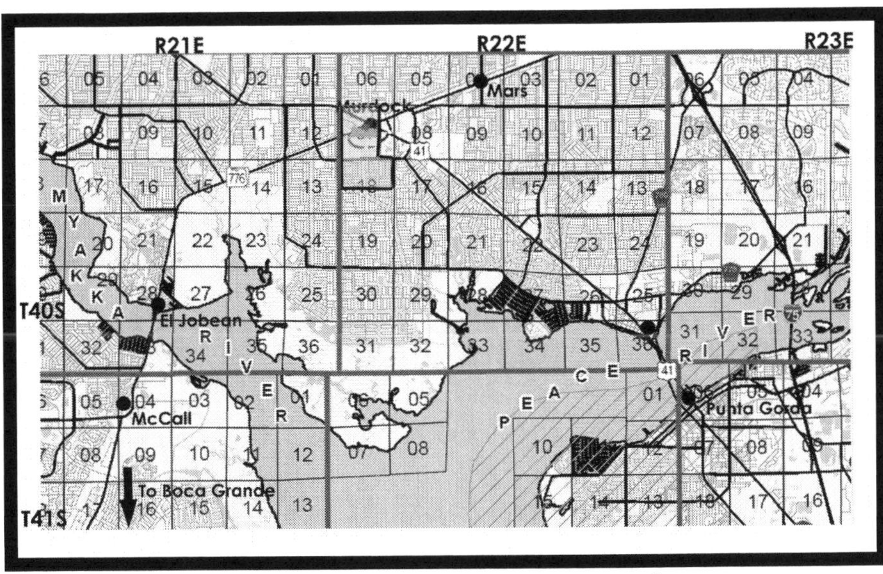

Granddaddy's Turpentine Lease Land
(Charlotte County Section Map Transformed).

With this lease, Granddaddy began his first turpentine operation. Having watched other people in the area and learned from them, he commenced the bleeding of trees and the boiling of the resin for turpentine. Family lore says that he paid small fees to the sheriff for leased convicts to do the work.

The leasing of convicts was a common practice in the state of Florida at the time. One such lease by another local operator required him to feed and clothe the convict and to pay the county eighty-five dollars per year for his labor.[1]

The practice of leasing convicts had continued in Florida, even after the state outlawed it in 1919 and simultaneously replaced it by legislative act with peonage, in spite of the Peonage Abolition Act of 1867 that was upheld by the Supreme Court in a Florida case in 1905. Peonage, defined as forced labor, allowed the turpentine bosses to recruit non-convict workers, charge them for transportation to the work sites and for ongoing supplies, and then hold them to work for a debt that could never be repaid.

The week after his turpentine lease began, the 1920 census indicates that Granddaddy was still working as a railroad agent, but he would not be for long. One day when the president of the railroad stopped by ahead of schedule to check on him, he caught Granddaddy working on his farm, gave him one week's notice, and ended his railroad career.

> January 19, 1920, Atlanta Constitution
> FANCY, bright oranges, $2.60 per box:
> A. C. Frizzell, Murdock, Fla.

Two months later, Granny became Murdock postmistress, with a commission beginning on March 10, 1920. She replaced Daniel Child, who had been postmaster for two and a half years.

Then on May 28, she and Granddaddy bought the post office and the Murdock general store, which were located on two and a half acres of land. They paid $600 for their first purchase in the area.

They opened the store, called it the Murdock Mercantile, and they stocked it well. They stocked it with locally grown produce, eggs, and chickens, with yard goods, clothing, shoes and shoe polish, hats, leather saddles and bridles, utensils, pocket knives, fly swatters, rat cheese, and food staples such as salt, sugar, sardines, crackers, and soft drinks including Coca Cola.

Granny and Granddaddy (Granny's Photo Album).

The Mercantile was an immediate success, being the only convenient place to shop for the hundreds of people who lived in the surrounding woods. Loggers and cowmen regularly shopped there, as well as men who hunted for a living and many others who worked on neighboring farms and turpentine plantations. The Murdock woods were alive with all kinds of people who spent their earnings at the Mercantile.

Granddaddy said that they eventually "took in as much as $75,000 a year from the store," and they invested it all in land. Granny did not trust banks, and Granddaddy knew that "someday a main highway would run through here."[2]

In August, Granddaddy assigned his turpentine lease to Weeks and Stephens. They were turpentine operators in the nearby pine woods to the west. They paid Granddaddy $2,400 for the lease. The lease had originally cost him $800, and so he made $1,600 on the transfer eight months later.

The following month, for $100 each, Granddaddy bought two two-and-a-half-acre parcels adjacent to the Mercantile and post office. The Murdock Hotel and the boarding house were located on the new parcels, and so perhaps there was more money involved than indicated on the deed, as was and is more often the case than not. He and Granny then moved into the boarding house and opened it to accommodate men in charge of nearby big lumbering operations and turpentine plantations. Two years later, they opened the hotel, where they would host social events and provide the occasional traveler respite from the dirt and dust, mosquitoes, and alligators that plagued those who dared to venture into the wilds of Southwest Florida.

The below map is an inset of the aqua rectangular area on the previous section map. It shows the platted town of Murdock and the Mercantile/Post Office and Hotel/Boarding House parcels. In less than three years, Granddaddy and Granny had acquired all four of the buildings that they had seen when they first stepped off the train in Murdock.

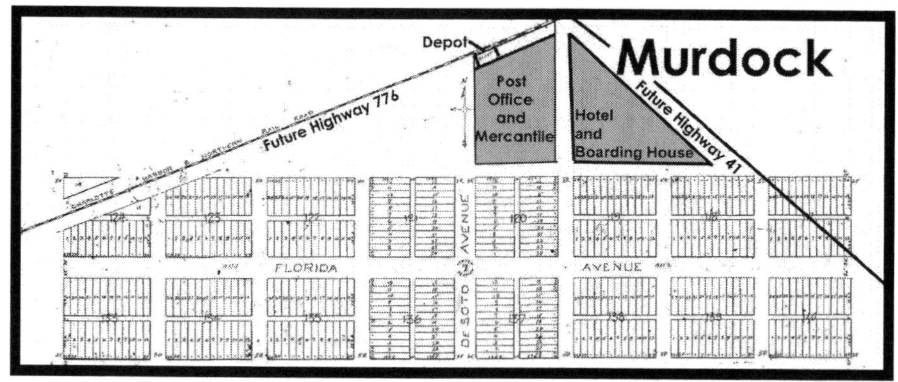

Frizzell Property 1920
(1914 Murdock Plat Map Transformed).

With the purchase of the Mercantile, the post office, the Murdock Hotel with eighteen or twenty rooms, and the sixteen-room boarding house, Granny's responsibilities multiplied. She had started as postmistress managing the post office, and now while Granddaddy was farming, she would also manage the Mercantile, the hotel, the boarding house, and all of their financial records.

Some folks believed that Granny was the driving force behind the Frizzell success story. She was brilliant, she managed their Murdock businesses, did all of their bookkeeping, and controlled their finances. Lore has it that when she was too old and too sick to work any longer, it took five bookkeepers to replace her.

Granny's control was not limited to finances; it extended to people, as well, including Granddaddy. When she told somebody what to do, that person did it. She once described her control mildly by saying that she kept "a restraining hand on Mr. Frizzell when he needed it."[3]

But nobody kept "a restraining hand" on Mrs. Frizzell, and when she heard the exciting news of August 18, 1920, she was off to the races. The 19th Amendment to the U. S. Constitution had granted American women the right to vote.

Florida had been the only state to take no action on the amendment, but it did allow women to vote, because the amendment invalidated existing state law. Florida men stood firm, though, and did not ratify the amendment until 1969. Women belonged at home, not "de-elevated" by the lowly, dirty business of politics. Along the same line, married women were allowed to own property, but they were not allowed to manage it, unless their husbands were incapacitated.

Women were not the only ones oppressed by the white male population of the state of Florida in the early 1900s. The blacks were struggling for their rights, too, which struggling included the inalienable rights to life, liberty, and the pursuit of happiness. They may have had the *right* to those rights, but they did not have the rights.

Although Florida was one of the least populated states east of the Mississippi River, it was probably the most oppressive with nearly half of its population being black. From 1900 to 1930, Florida trailed only Alabama and Mississippi in total number of lynchings, but outranked them both in per capita lynchings.

As for voting rights, Florida was the first state to adopt a poll tax (1889) that deliberately blocked poor folks, in particular blacks, from voting. The tax was $2.00 annually, and it was not abolished until 1937. Proof of poll tax payment had to be presented to a poll clerk who was appointed for each precinct to manage the polling place.

Murdock's poll clerk for the November 1920 election would be Granddaddy, and a week after he was appointed in October, Granny entered the race for a local public office, only two months after women were granted the right to vote. The woman who had expertly been managing businesses for many years and continued to do so, at a time and in a place where women were not allowed to manage their own property, became DeSoto County's first woman candidate.

"The race of De Soto County's first woman candidate will be watched with interest and add ginger to the election in old DeSoto."

October 15, 1920

WOMAN CANDIDATE FOR CLERK CIRCUIT COURT
MRS. PATTIE B. FRIZZELL
WILL OPPOSE DEMOCRATIC NOMINEE

Wauchula - Desoto County is to have a woman candidate for the office of clerk of the circuit court in the coming election. Mrs. Pattie B. Frizzell of Murdock appeared before the county commissioners in Arcadia Wednesday with a duly signed petition asking that her name be placed on the ticket as a candidate for clerk of the circuit court.

Mrs. Frizzell is a business woman. For two years she was station agent for the Charlotte Harbor and Northern Railroad Company at Ona, and for six months was manager of the Western Union office in Wauchula. Mrs. Frizzell had charge of the telegraph office during Wauchula's greatest truck season and handled the large volume of business in a manner which won the praise of all.

While by no means old [age 49], Mrs. Frizzell is a woman who has had much business experience. She was born and reared in Alabama and has been in DeSoto county for six years. [Ona was also in DeSoto County at the time.]

The regular Democratic nominee for the office is A. L. Durrance, who has held the office for two terms and was an easy victor in the late primary.

The race of DeSoto County's first woman candidate will be watched with interest and add ginger to the election in old DeSoto.

October 24, 1920, ARCADIA column
Mrs. P. B. Frizzell of Murdock, candidate for clerk of the circuit court, was in town yesterday in the interest of her candidacy, and she was in Bowling Green Friday making herself known to the voters.

October 28, 1920, Punta Gorda Herald
To the Voters of DeSoto County:
I wish to place my name before the voters of this county as a candidate for the office of Clerk of the Circuit Court. In doing this, I am sensible of the fact that I should make some sort of an explanation of my action, and to give those who do not know me some information concerning myself.

I was born and raised a democrat, and have always believed in the principles of that party. I was unable to get my name before the people in the primary, because, at that time, the women of the country were not recognized as citizens. Since that time, however, the nation has granted to women their long delayed rights, and as a democrat I have been placed on the ticket as an independent. I am not an independent, in fact, but a democrat, and if it had been possible I would have been in the race in the June primary.

I have a good education, both classical and business, and have been in responsible positions for years and have handled such business work as manager of the Western Union Telegraph offices in Arcadia, Wauchula and important cities, as well as managing the affairs of the Murdock Mercantile Company. I am thoroughly conversant with the duties of the clerk of the court and promise, if I am selected by the people to fill this office, that I will give faithful and efficient service at all times. I realize the importance of this office, which concerns the business affairs of the county, records, deeds, etc., and will give the people the very best I can bring to the office in painstaking and careful service. I solicit your support and influence.

MRS. P. B. FRIZZELL, Murdock, Florida

Granny did not win, but she made a good showing, considering both the time in history and the fact that she was running against a popular male incumbent who had held the position for two terms. She lost 110 to 191. Of interest is that all of her votes were supposedly cast by women.

In the spring of the following year, on April 4, 1921, Granny "consented" to the marriage of Annabel, then age 21, to Henry Cuthbert "Buster" Mathis, age 26. The 1920 census indicates that Buster was living with his mother Pearl in a rented house in Wauchula. He had served in the U. S. Navy on the sea in World War I, and afterward worked as a salesman for a drug store.

Annabel moved to Wauchula, where she and Buster would live for the rest of their lives. Annabel would work as a lawyer's stenographer, a court reporter, and a real estate broker with an office in their home on one of the main streets of Wauchula; Buster would continue working as a salesman. They would have one daughter, Martha Pearle, named for her two grandmothers.

By the time that Annabel and Buster settled into their new married life in Wauchula, they were living in a new county. On April 23, the Florida House of Representatives passed a bill dividing DeSoto into five counties: Charlotte, DeSoto, Glades, Hardee, and Highlands. Wauchula would be the seat for Hardee County, and Punta Gorda would be the seat for Charlotte County, Murdock's new county.

Charlotte County extended from the Gulf of Mexico to about 45 miles inland and stretched about 20 miles north and south from Sarasota and DeSoto counties to Lee County, for a total of almost 900 square miles.

With the exception of El Jobean and a few privately owned parcels, Granddaddy and Granny eventually owned the Charlotte County land between the Myakka and Peace Rivers (about twenty miles wide colored green on the below map). Their holdings also extended into

Punta Gorda and beyond in all directions, as well as across the Myakka River to the west, into Sarasota and DeSoto Counties to the north, and Lee County to the south.

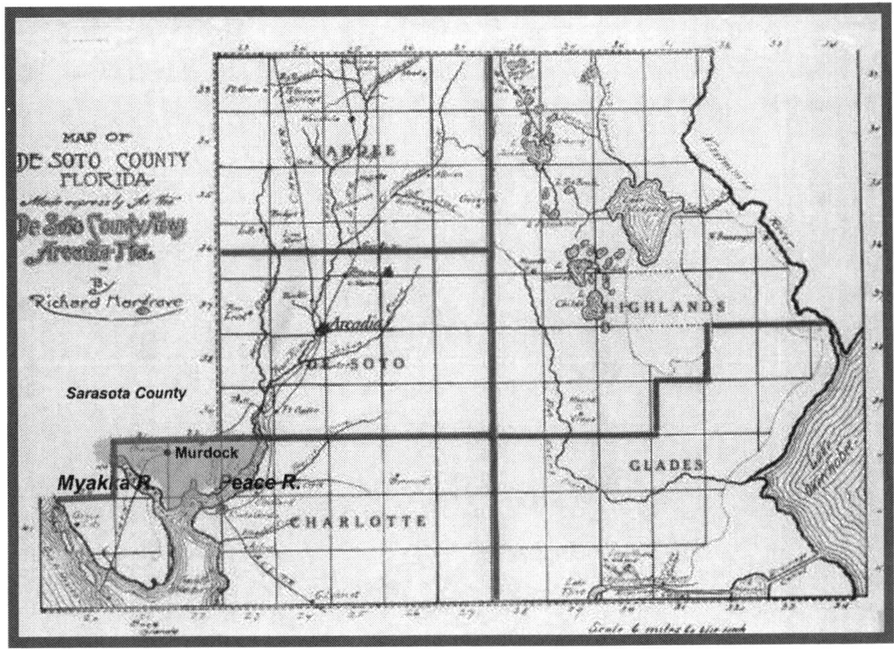

Map of Desoto County, Florida. 1921.
Black & white photoprint, 8 x 10 in. State Archives of Florida, Florida Memory. <https://www.floridamemory.com/items/show/39608>, (accessed 22 March 2018).

The very next day after the county division, Granddaddy and Granny motored to Englewood and spent the day with Mr. and Mrs. A. Stanley Lampp, no doubt discussing their new county. Stanley Lampp owned a hotel in Englewood, and he was a big property owner there.

By this time, Florida's Land Boom was going strong, and new buildings had already begun springing up in Punta Gorda, when the Hagan-Whitten Bridge opened across the Peace River a couple of months later on July 4th, 1921. It was a mile long and fourteen feet wide, with a speed limit of fifteen miles per hour. Financed by public subscription, it epitomized American independence and appropriately opened on the day of its celebration.

Granddaddy and Granny probably joined about 6,000 other folks from miles around to drive across the bridge for the first time and attend a dedication ceremony at the bandstand in Gilchrist Park on the bay. After a free public fish fry that included swamp cabbage, they watched fireworks over their new bridge to the future.

Punta Gorda Bridge - Punta Gorda, Florida. 1925.
Black & white photoprint, 8 x 10 in. State Archives of Florida, Florida Memory. <https://www.floridamemory.com/items/show/36957>, (accessed 26 April 2018).

Less than four months later, on October 25, the milestone bridge would prove its strength and stand firm against the Tampa Bay Hurricane, which made landfall at Tarpon Springs. The Category 3 hurricane was the worst to affect the Tampa Bay region in seventy years. Although the hurricane hit over 100 miles to the north, the storm tide reached seven feet above normal in Charlotte County, where the elevation varies, but averages about four feet above sea level.

The high water of Charlotte Harbor probably covered the bridge, and it spilled into the streets of Punta Gorda, flooding the town. Water in the streets reached two to four feet high, and people rowed their boats from one place to another.

In Murdock, most of 400 acres of vegetables drowned. The truck farmers replanted, but floods came, and the vegetables again drowned. The persistent truck farmers continued replanting and expected profitable prices in the end.

In spite of the floods, by January of that season, truck farming assumed some importance in Murdock for the first time in several years. Various farmers were busy planting and reported that winter cool snaps had not hurt the truck so far.

Granddaddy planted cabbage, tomatoes, peppers, watermelons, and cucumbers. This was after successfully harvesting two and a half acres of cane from which he made 1,140 gallons of syrup and proceeded to plant an additional eight acres of cane.

Harvesting Cabbages at Murdock Farms Colony
Charlotte Harbor Area Historical Society and U.S. Cleveland
http://ccflhistory.contentdm.oclc.org/cdm/ref/collection/p15007coll1/id/432,
(accessed April 26, 2018).

Granddaddy stocked the Mercantile with his farm goods, as well with those of his neighbors, among them Daniel Child. One of Daniel's first diary entries tells how he sold twenty-seven pounds of sweet potatoes and three dozen eggs at the Mercantile. About a month later, he sold four roosters for 25 cents per pound – coming to $4.25.

At the time of his first diary, Daniel was age 46 and living alone. His 26-year-old wife Nora had left for England with their son Charles, and they would never return. Daniel would live the remainder of his years alone in Murdock.

That summer of 1922 brought Granddaddy's parents Joe and Blanche, his brothers Johnnie, age 22, and Roy, age 14, and his sister Lula, age 23, to Murdock from Alabama. They may have arrived for a visit, but they all stayed and lived with Granddaddy and Granny in the boarding house.

At about that same time, a young man named Tilley Irvin Kennedy, age 18, started working as a telegrapher for the railroad in Murdock. When Lula met Tilley, it was love at first sight and the reason she stayed in Murdock, although she said she stayed to help Granny in the Mercantile. A year later, she and Tilley married, had a brief honeymoon, and lived together in the boarding house.

In July, Granddaddy and his brother Johnnie took off by car for a four-week vacation to Birmingham, Alabama, and as soon as they returned, Granddaddy bought his second of many tax deed properties. For $38.51, he bought all twenty-four lots of Block 140 in Murdock. Two years before, he had bought his first tax deed property. For $33.78, he had bought all twenty-four lots of Block 120 in Murdock.

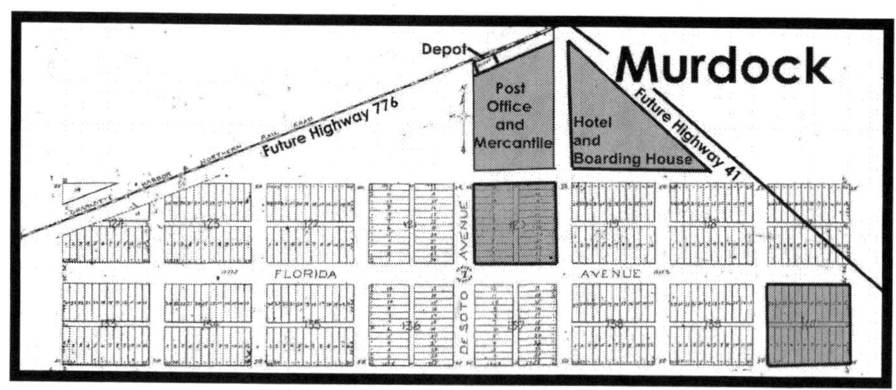

Frizzell Property 1922
(1914 Murdock Plat Map Transformed).

September that year brought rains so heavy that by the end of the month, the teacher was unable to get to the schoolhouse, and the kids had a two-day holiday. Most of the children had managed to make it there, but they were very glad the teacher did not appear.

A neighbor told Daniel Child that he had "ridden the wood ever since '79" and never saw so much water before. He called the rain a "frog strangler."

A Murdock resident wrote *The Tampa Tribune*:

> Won't somebody please go to see the weather man and offer him some inducement that will make him call off the rains for awhile and save some of the water until next spring when we will be very likely to need it?

The C. H. & N. carpenter crew appeared one day and made some very badly needed repairs caused by rain damage to the depot and section houses, but nobody was doing anything to repair the area's bad roads that were getting worse by the minute.

While Murdock's farmers were busy trying to get ready for their fall plantings, one of their wives complained about the roads in the *Punta Gorda Herald*:

> We are tired of staying at home, and so we are. We want to go to Punta Gorda, to the movies, and we want some ice cream, and we want to go – oh! We just want to go, to be going somewhere; and if the roads are not fixed so that we can go, and not be half dead when we get back home, we are going to persuade our husbands to sell out and move somewhere where the roads are good and we can go to town. So that's that.

Back in January, Granddaddy and 255 other Charlotte County residents had petitioned for a special election to authorize the issue of county bonds in an amount sufficient to make needed repairs to old roads and to open and construct such new roads as would meet the needs and wishes of the people of all sections of the county. Everybody in Murdock was heartily in favor of the bond issue, the road between Murdock and Punta Gorda being extremely rough.

In response to the petition, Charlotte County voters approved a $150,000 bond issue to complete their section of the Tamiami Trail, a road that would connect Tampa and Miami and would include Road No. 5, which connected Murdock and Punta Gorda. The idea of the Tamiami Trail had been conceived in 1914, and construction had begun in 1915, with each community being responsible for its own section.

When work finally started in Charlotte County, Granddaddy donated work crews and mules to help complete the road and open up the area. Completion would mean a road sixteen feet wide and surfaced with brick or some other comparable material.

With the advent of new and improved roads, the Florida Land Boom started spreading from Punta Gorda to other parts of Charlotte County, in particular to the sleepy fishing camp of El Jobean, then called Southland and known for its turtle-canning plant. Southland was located on the Myakka River, eight miles southwest of Murdock on the future Highway 776 that leads to the Gulf of Mexico.

The history of Southland is revealed by the graves in Southland Trail Cemetery (called "Convict Cemetery" by locals). Early graves before 1870 contain the remains of Cuban fishermen who lived there in palmetto-thatched-roof huts. Graves from 1870 to 1923 are unmarked and contain the remains of leased convicts (most imprisoned under the Jim Crowe laws) who worked at turpentine and lumber camps in the area.

"Convict Cemetery," 2010.

While funding was being approved for Highway 41, a Boston attorney named Joel Bean discovered Southland and envisioned great potential for its future. He bought approximately 4,000 acres of land there that fronted on the Myakka River for four and a half miles. The land was originally part of federal lands that were deeded to the state of Florida in 1850.

Then in 1922, he built a post office/general store with a back door facing the railroad track that paralleled the future Highway 776, and he began construction of the El Jobean Grand Hotel and Fishing Lodge across the street. The hotel would have a total of twenty-four guest rooms, two bathrooms, two front rooms that were used as a lobby with one fireplace, a hotel office, a kitchen with a fireplace, and a dining room.

El Jobean Post Office/Depot, Built 1922,
listed in the National Register of Historic Places, photo 2010.

A museum inside the building,
the old post office window with bars, in front left of photo, 2010.

On a table inside the museum, a model of Joel Bean's Grand Hotel, 2010.

The front of Joel Bean's Grand Hotel and Fishing Lodge in 2010.

The next year in 1923, Joel Bean recorded a plat for a "City of Destiny," which he named El Jobean, a Spanish-sounding anagram of his name. He divided El Jobean into seven wards, each with its own civic center on a plaza with residential lots encircling it. It was the first city platted in the round. Murdock is located at the intersection at the upper far right edge of the map.

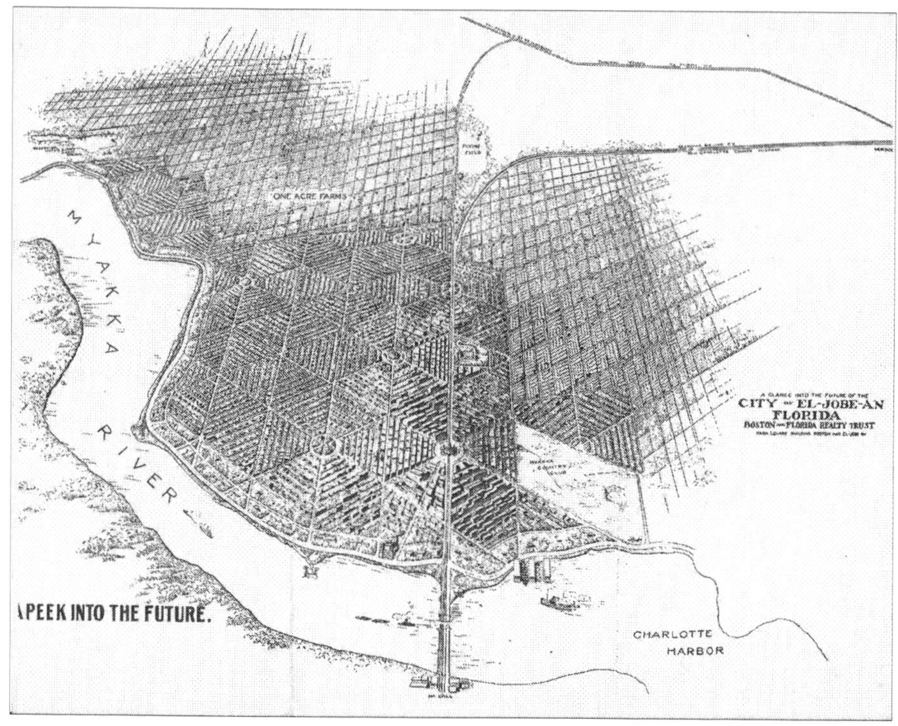

With his plat in hand, he then returned to Boston, where he printed beautiful brochures and sold hundreds of residential lots in paradise to unsuspecting Bostonians. The poetically-written brochures did not mention that there were no streets to most of the lots, which were located in the woods in the middle of nowhere. Nor did the brochures mention that Ward 4 was almost entirely a swamp, knee-deep in water with nothing but saw grass growing there. What the brochures did mention was that El Jobean was once the proud possession of the Duke of Myakka, whoever he was.

Excerpts from Joel Bean's brochure follow.

EL – JOBE - AN
A City In The Making

NATURE fashioned myriad picture spots, then she came to Florida to paint her masterpiece. She drew from a million widespread triumphs to tip her brush with the brilliant colors that have given Florida rare qualities of beauty, and to invigorate her paints with a climate that has builded health, happiness and prosperity.

One traverses a far-flung Union of enchanting States and settles in Florida to enjoy the health and beauty of that State to which Nature turned to spread her most lavish endowments.

It fell to the happy lot of the West Coast to receive the choicest triumphs that Nature drew from her bag of rich beauties and opportunities, and it has been the good fortune of EL-JOBE-AN to stand in the West Coast's most select spot, at the head of Charlotte Harbor, in the heart of a fertile country, in a district of easy access, ready markets and superb business opportunities ...

No better place in all of Florida could have been selected as the site of a future tourist and commercial city than on the banks of this wonderful river where it enters Charlotte Harbor. On this land which was once the proud possession of the Duke of Myakka a city is being built, unrivalled in beauty of arrangement and unapproached in ideal surroundings...

EL-JOBE-AN conjured from Nature's most exquisite pattern, spreads her earnest welcome to climes of pleasant warmth and scenes of noble beauty, A City in the Making, nourished by a smiling sun that gives fruit and flower to its trees and rest and comfort to its visitors...

> We don't expect the "doubting Thomas" to listen to or take advantage of this unfolding opportunity, so we pass him up without argument. To the progressive, foresighted men and women, who have faith in themselves, as well as faith in others, we dedicate EL-JOBE-AN and offer them the opportunity of a life time...
>
> Our prices and terms are not equalled in all Florida for this class of property. Prices range from $350 upwards. A small cash payment and the balance in small monthly payments will secure a lot in EL-JOBE-AN. There are no strings to these terms ... Make your slogan, "buy a lot of lots at EL-JOBE-AN," while prices are low and terms easy.

Soon, the small village area of El Jobean started attracting visitors and settlers, but because of its remoteness, it attracted those who lived by their own codes and sought a place where they could do so without notice. It attracted members of Al Capone's gang, and it attracted early entertainment pioneers of Florida, in particular circus, carnival, and show people.

It attracted Elizabeth Adams, heiress to the Adams Chewing Gum Company, and probably El Jobean's most notable early settler. In the 1920s, she built herself a two-story mansion that overlooked the river about a block from the hotel. It dwarfed the small, white frame houses that were populating the village.

The Adams Chewing Gum Company, famous for Chiclets, had installed the first vending machines in the United States. In 1888, the machines debuted on the elevated subway platforms of New York City and offered one piece of gum for one penny.

Toward the end of October 1922, while Joel Bean was busy conjuring up his fantasy city of El Jobean, the rain finally slacked, and Murdock sprang back to life. The "Country Lasses" all piled into the back of Milton Roberts' little Ford truck, and he hauled them all over town, until the truck got stuck in the muck. Then for Halloween, the older school children gave a party at the schoolhouse with refreshments, ghosts, goblins, black cats, witches, and a warning to the little folks to be careful and not let the goblins get them. That following Sunday, Granny got on her prohibition bandwagon at Sunday School with an earnest talk in favor of temperance and told of her own experience with the "demon rum."

The month of November then began with the mysterious death of hogs on many of the Murdock farms, including Granddaddy's, and an election day with Granny serving as poll clerk and Granddaddy as Deputy Sheriff. In keeping with Florida Statutes, the Sheriff had deputized Granddaddy to maintain peace and good order at the polling place. A total of eleven votes were cast in Murdock, with Granny being the only woman voter, although several more were eligible.

Soon after election day, Granddaddy and Granny used canal-bank clay to build up the front yard of the Murdock Hotel, and they opened it for business, after several months of preparation. They renamed it Stanzell Lodge, Stanzell surely being a contraction of Granny's previous married name, Standifer, and Frizzell.

They expected the lodge to attract many visitors to the area. It was centrally located, near enough to Big Slough for sportsmen to go there for a day of fishing and near enough to Salt Springs for those seeking health-giving water to go and return in half a day. Its opening would, no doubt, give the village of Murdock a boost.

One of their first guests was a J. G. Lewis of Jacksonville, who was there on business. While having lunch at the lodge, he tasted some of the local honey and liked it so much that he purchased seven gallons and shipped it to Jacksonville for his family table.

J. G. Lewis was probably there for turpentine business at the Murdock camps. He was president of the Baldwin-Lewis Company in Jacksonville, and he advertised "Naval Stores, Factors and Wholesale Grocers, Turpentine Supplies by A Factorage House Managed by Practical Turpentine Men, The Patronage of Those Having Desirable Accounts Solicited."

About a week after the hotel opened, Daniel Child wrote that Granddaddy was "harrowing and said he would like to get me to clip his 2 mules tomorrow." They agreed on a price of $1.50 each, and Daniel asked his friend Charley to help.

> Had breakfast nearly ready when Charley came with the pair of Frizzell mules at 8. At 8:30, we began clipping. We got Jack clipped in 2 hours 43 minutes. He stood beautifully. Then we worked on Frank till 12:35 when we stopped for dinner. We took a few minutes over an hour for dinner and finished Frank at 3:15, making about 2 hours 55 minutes for Frank, who is finer haired, and we changed upper clipping plate on him. He also stood very well. The best pair of animals to stand I ever remember to have clipped, and Charley is fine at the crank.

A few days later, Daniel wrote that more than $32 had been taken a little at a time in the past month from the post office. Two boys had finally been caught. "They had made a wire hook, which they stuck through one of the empty mailboxes, hooked into the cash box, and drew it within reach and helped themselves to the change." Granny told Daniel that she would not prosecute the boys, "but their parents would have to take them in hand." She said that the matter would have to be reported to post office authorities.

Soon after the robbery case was solved, Granny took off to Tampa for two weeks, probably to visit her dear friend, Mrs. Hiram Hart, and she missed a big yellow bus passing through Murdock at 8:30 one morning. It was making the inauguration run of a "jitney" service between Sarasota and Arcadia. The route would include Murdock and Punta Gorda. Many folks were hoping that its patronage would justify its existence.

Granny then returned from Tampa in time to host a Christmas Eve dinner at Stanzell Lodge. She and Granddaddy invited Daniel and Charley, as well as Annabel and her husband Buster. They sat down about 2:15 for a "fine fried chicken dinner with dessert, coffee, and all the fixins." Afterward, they went to a "preaching service," and the next day, Granny gave Daniel a box of chocolates.

A couple of days later, Granddaddy asked Daniel to work for him in his cane. Daniel agreed, and he wrote details of the entire process in his diary.

Day 1. On Thursday, he cut cane, stripping and topping it, for six hours, with an hour break for dinner. He then helped Johnny Wetherington haul up seven truckloads of cane in a wagon to the mill.

The mill would have looked similar to the one in the below photo.

Small, John Kunkel, 1869-1938. *The boiling of cane syrup*. 1916?. Black & white glass photonegative, 5 x 7 in. State Archives of Florida, Florida Memory. <https://www.floridamemory.com/items/show/49276>, (accessed 19 December 2018).

Day 2. He worked another six hours. In the morning, he helped Johnny haul up three more loads of cane, and then they ground the cane with a gas engine; in the afternoon, they began cooking it down. He helped Charley feed the mill, until the juice started boiling. Then, he took away the bagasse, and Charley fed the mill alone. Bagasse is the pulpy residue left after extraction of the juice from the cane.

Daniel did not work on Saturday, and on Sunday, he taught the adult class at Sunday School. He said that in a general discussion after the lesson, Granny talked about how well the Murdock people always take care of the sick and how she was never too busy to throw down her work and go to attend a sick person.

Day 3. On Tuesday, it was back to the grind. Daniel worked five hours and 40 minutes. In addition to Granddaddy, Charley, and Johnny, the cane gang now included "Ada, colored, and her about ten-year-old daughter." Daniel helped Johnny haul six more truckloads of cane. For the last hour or so, they cut cane on the north patch. The cane was very big there. At the end of the day, Daniel took 200 sugar cane tops home to feed his cattle. Sugar cane tops were used for cattle feed, although they were low in nutritive value.

Day 4. It was the same gang as the day before, but with three more added. One was out with a wagon and mules, plowing the fields, while another and his son worked the evaporator (a set of boiling pans), making the syrup. Daniel carried away bagasse for five hours. That evening, he took his cattle another 100 tops.

Day 5. He worked for five hours mowing. Granddaddy had told him the day before to bring his mowing machine, and Daniel had agreed to rent it to him for a dollar per day, besides replacement of any breakage. He was to drive it with Granddaddy's mules, but he had to use his own two horses to take it there. "Mr. Frizzell had several new hands, colored today, and Walter was back."

Day 6. Daniel cut cane until noon and then mowed.

Day 7. Off for the weekend and back to work Monday for three hours of mowing.

Day 8. On Wednesday, they "wound up the syrup-making for the season." After cooking off the last juice in the evaporator, the last gallon was too trashy to filter, and so Granddaddy gave it to Daniel. Daniel also got a little that would not go in the cans and the scrapings of the two tubs. He walked home in order to carry it in a water bucket. After supper, he worked it on the stove with two frying pans, diluting it first in order to filter it. He got a gallon of syrup, besides "skimmings."

Granddaddy calculated the run at 650 gallons. It had taken an average of a half a dozen workers eight days, from field to evaporator, to produce 650 gallons of sugar cane syrup.

A couple of weeks after the sugar cane run, Aunt Lula rang in the new year 1923 with a party by the light of a big bonfire in front of the Mercantile. She passed around homemade peanut candy and roasted peanuts to about twenty adults and young people. Then, they all played games. They played Marching 'Round the Level and Miller's Boy, which were circle-form singing games like Ring Around the Rosie, and they played Quack, a singing hand game.

Daniel, who attended the party, wrote that it ended about midnight. He doused the fire with two cans of water, and he helped Aunt Lula home with the leftover candy.

> March 1, 1923
> "FOR SALE – One Master truck 2 ½ tons capacity.
> Used one orange season. Practically new, $1,250.
> A. C. Frizzell, Murdock, Fla."

The truck would have looked similar to the 1921 Master truck pictured below and described as "Master of the Load on any Road."

Starting in May, Granddaddy bought a total of 160 acres during the next year, and in September, he renewed his turpentine lease. The 160 acres was a block of land divided by the future Highway 41 about a mile and a half southeast of Murdock. The renewed turpentine lease, he would transfer to Henry Evans and net $300 on the deal in a matter of days.

There were two big events in 1923. The first occurred on July 25, when at the recommendation of the county Democratic committee, Governor Hardee appointed Granddaddy county commissioner to replace a commissioner who had resigned. The second big event was the installation of electric lights in the Mercantile and at Stanzell Lodge. Two evenings after the lights were installed at the lodge, Granny held a radiophone concert there and invited neighbors to hear it. It was their first such concert, and they stayed until 11:30.

There were two big events in 1924, too. The first was a terrible accident, and the second was a pivotal real estate deal.

The first event occurred on September 6, when Granddaddy was feeding gasoline from a bucket to the intake manifold of an engine on his farm. The engine backfired and ignited the gasoline in the bucket. Granddaddy immediately hurled the bucket, unaware that a machinist named Matt Weeks was standing in its path. The flaming fuel burned the entire length of Matt's right leg, sent him to the doctor in Punta Gorda, and prevented him from working for several weeks. His injury could have been much worse, had he not the presence of mind to throw himself on the ground and holler for onlookers to smother him with sand.[4]

The second event began on October 31, when the owners of Granddaddy's turpentine lease property signed an agreement for him to act as exclusive agent to sell all of their Murdock land that totaled 2,368 acres. They wanted $14.25 per acre, and he was to receive anything over that amount. Two months later on December 20, he sold the land for $1,000 down at $18 per acre, which meant that he made $8,880 on the deal (about $100,000 today).

By this time, Charlotte County's boom was at its peak. Granddaddy and Granny had re-opened the Murdock Hotel the year before, and Joel Bean had finished building the El Jobean Grand Hotel and Fishing Lodge. Now, Punta Gorda needed someone to re-open its landmark hotel that had closed in 1914.

The Hotel Punta Gorda had been built there in 1887 by the Florida Southern Railroad in order to attract passengers to its most southern terminal in the U. S. Although the hotel was one of the first buildings in the area, it attracted over 3,300 guests that first season when it opened in January 1888.

In spite of its isolation, the area then easily became a popular destination resort, frequented by many distinguished visitors, such as Winston Churchill, Samuel Colt, Clarence Darrow, Thomas Edison, Harvey Firestone, Henry Ford, Teddy Roosevelt, and W.K. Vanderbilt.

They were all attracted to the winter climate and to the tarpon fishing, with the exception of Teddy Roosevelt the adventurer. He was more attracted to the local manta rays and managed to land one over sixteen feet wide, which ranked second in size to the world record at the time.

The area's distinguished visitors normally arrived either by yacht or by private rail car, and most of them stayed at the Hotel Punta Gorda. A pier stretched into the harbor in front of the hotel for yachts, and a track ran along the side of the hotel for private rail cars. Traveling theater groups often arrived by private rail car, too, and used the same track, but they stayed at a nearby more modest hotel.

Hotel Punta Gorda - Punta Gorda, Florida. Not before 1880.
Black & white photoprint, 5 x 7 in. State Archives of Florida, Florida Memory.
<https://www.floridamemory.com/items/show/118064>,
(accessed 26 April 2018).

The three-story Hotel Punta Gorda was listed in a Guide to the Best Hotels in the World, 1894-1895. It boasted "150 fine rooms." They were among the most luxurious in the state of Florida with gas, electric bells, and open fireplaces, and they all overlooked Charlotte Harbor, the tarpon fishing capital of the world. The ad described the hotel's "superb two-acre lawn, with shell walks, flower-beds, shade and fruit trees" in a "perfect climate, with warmth tempered by salt-water breezes from the Gulf of Mexico."[5]

PUNTA GORDA, Florida, U. S.—Hotel Punta Gorda.

On Charlotte Harbor.

150 Fine Rooms. Veranda, 400 feet long. Superb two-acre lawn, with shell walks, flower-beds, shade and fruit trees.

Perfect climate, with warmth tempered by salt-water breezes from the Gulf of Mexico.

The finest tarpon fishing in the world, with competent guides; row and sail boats, and naphtha launches. Fine shooting.

. . . Hotel Refurnished. . . .
Gas. Electric Bells. Open Fire-Places.

HARRY B. WARDEN, *Manager.*

In March 1894, an ad also appeared in *Forest and Stream* and said that the hotel "Is now open for the reception of guests. Splendid shooting and fishing. Special rates to families. Through parlor car from Jacksonville to hotel door."

The Charlotte Harbor ferry dock can be seen in the forefront of both of the above photos.

The hotel stayed open for twenty-six years until it closed in 1914; then it stayed closed for ten years, until Barron Collier came along during the boom. Barron Collier was an advertising entrepreneur who became one of Florida's largest landowners. He bought the Hotel Punta Gorda and changed its name to the Hotel Charlotte Harbor. He remodeled it and expanded the grounds. He added a fourth floor ballroom, a boat basin, and an Olympic-size swimming pool. He stuccoed the exterior and added arches, giving it a Spanish appearance.

About the time that Barron Collier finished renovating the Hotel Charlotte Harbor, the Tamiami Trail was near completion, three years after Granddaddy had first volunteered mules and crews. On June 19, 1925, *The Tampa Tribune* reported, "The road from Sarasota to Punta Gorda is in good condition now with the exception of an eight mile detour between Punta Gorda and Murdock. The new road from the Myakka River to Murdock, a distance of eleven miles, is excellent, having just been completed. The road contractors report that the entire road to Punta Gorda will be completed and ready for traffic in less than sixty days."

Hotel Charlotte Harbor [new look] - Punta Gorda, Florida. 192-.
Black & white photonegative, 4 x 5 in. State Archives of Florida, Florida Memory.
<https://www.floridamemory.com/items/show/146587>, (accessed 26 April 2018).

The Tamiami Bus Line was operating from Sarasota to Fort Myers, and the bus operators were receiving compliments on their service. The fifty-mile trip from Sarasota to Punta Gorda took three hours, compared to one full long day by horse and buggy.

> June 25, 1925
> WANTED - White woman, combined cook and housekeeper for boarding house. Salary fourteen dollars per week and room and board.
> Mrs. A. C. Frizzell, Stanzell Lodge, Murdock, Fla."

The completion of the Tamiami Trail opened the doors of the Hotel Charlotte Harbor to highway travelers and, at the same time, it opened new doors of opportunity to Granddaddy that extended far beyond Murdock. Now that he could easily travel by car, he would expand his holdings and operations over the years to include: land throughout five counties; two lumber companies and the Ford Place in Punta Gorda; a tractor dealership, a third lumber company, a hardware store, a drug store, and a music store in Ft. Myers; and many others, including sawmills and ranches scattered all over the place.

Now that the area was open to the future by a highway, Granddaddy bought his first really large tract of land. He bought it from Benjamin Franklin Yoakum, chairman of the board of directors of the Frisco Railroad. Yoakum had planned to purchase the C. H. & N. and extensively develop the Murdock area, but Seaboard Air Line leased the railroad in 1925, and so Yoakum liquidated his Murdock holdings.[6]

Separate from the Yoakum tract, Granddaddy recorded twenty-eight land transactions in the Charlotte County courthouse in 1925. He did a lot of buying and profitable quick re-selling, in particular, but not limited to, Murdock homesteads. He also continued buying platted lots in Murdock, acreage parcels, and tax deed property. Thanks to the Florida 1920s real estate boom, he was well on his way.

Granddaddy said that he and Granny did not plan to acquire so much property. "We just naturally wanted land that adjoined ours."[7]

Granddaddy and Granny

The completion of the Tamiami Trail opened one other door for Granddaddy. It opened the side door of Mack and Ma McGraw's Acline Wine Place with its famous moonshine whiskey and wild women. Located on Alligator Creek on Highway 41 south of Punta

Gorda, it was a convenient stop for Granddaddy when he traveled to Punta Gorda and Ft. Myers to oversee his various operations.

Although Prohibition had been in effect for five years since January 1920 and would be for another eight years, the Acline Wine Place never shut its side door, and Granddaddy became one of its regular evening customers. He was a big man, and he drank big. He drank a full bottle of "demon" alcohol every night, but he was up every morning at four o'clock ready for work.

While 54-year-old Granny sat in a rocking chair at home alone, preaching temperance to whomever would listen, 35-year-old Granddaddy sat on a straight-backed kitchen chair in Ma McGraw's scantily furnished front room that was packed full of other people sitting in kitchen chairs. There, he charmed the women, and he drank Ma's magic potion, which she called *wine*.

Other bars along the Tamiami Trail sold reputable moonshine whiskey, but none sold a drink that compared to Ma's *wine*. She had first concocted it for local teenage boys who passed into manhood at the Acline Wine Place. Because she did not believe that they should drink raw moonshine, she made a special brew for them in a galvanized tub. To one gallon of white lightning, she added one gallon of strawberry syrup that she bought at the Seminole Pharmacy soda fountain in Punta Gorda. She cut the mixture with creek water and stirred it with a broom. For the older, more discerning customer, she substituted smuggled import whiskey or cognac for the white lightning.

With the opening of the Tamiami Trail, the Acline Wine Place became famous throughout South Florida. Customers hailed from as far as Tampa and Miami. [8]

The Tamiami Trail also brought the Florida Highway Patrol to the area and the beginning of a long-standing feud. Granddaddy was accustomed to doing as he pleased, and he refused to follow the motor vehicle rules. He disobeyed the speed limits, he drove while intoxicated, and he wrecked almost every automobile that he ever owned. Family lore has it that he occasionally encouraged the blind eye of law enforcement officials with a gift of a half cow each to take home to their families, but he would still get himself into trouble, especially in later years.

December 22, 1925 **STRAYED OR STOLEN**

STOLEN from A. C. Frizzell, Murdock, Fla, Dec. 15, large male black and white collie, answers to name of Mack; liberal reward paid for information leading to his recovery or delivery to Murdock Mer. Co. store, Murdock, Fla.

During the first half of 1926, Granddaddy continued buying and selling real estate. His recorded deals included grants of rights-of-way to Florida Power and Light for poles and lines on his land along Highway 41.

He also finished building a new home. He and Granny left the boarding house after living there for six years and moved to their new permanent residence. It was an unpretentious, small white frame house with a long driveway leading to it from Highway 41 (where the Charlotte County Administration is today).

Frizzell Murdock Home
(Granny's Photo Album).

At the same time, the Baltimore Orioles moved into the Charlotte Bay Hotel in Punta Gorda and made it their spring home.

Eastward looking view of Marion Avenue [The Charlotte Bay Hotel] Punta Gorda, Florida. 1926.

Black & white photoprint, 8 x 10 in. State Archives of Florida, Florida Memory. <https://www.floridamemory.com/items/show/29002>, (accessed 26 April 2018).

The summer of 1926 ended with the Great Miami Hurricane on September 11. It killed 262 people, injured over 6,000, and stopped the economic boom in South Florida.

Although Punta Gorda was not directly hit, 120-mile-per-hour winds blew by just south of the town, and a storm surge left residents calmly rowing their boats in the streets, again. The high winds tore roofs off local businesses and destroyed six homes and the Episcopal Church. Not many homeowners carried windstorm insurance, but for those who did, the insurance companies only covered fifty percent of the value of the home.[9]

The storm ravaged Murdock, too. It damaged nearly every home there, blew the roof off the school, and destroyed the railroad depot. It damaged the citrus crop, as well. Residents raised a fund for storm relief, and Granny wrote *The Tampa Tribune* that she would temporarily care for or legally adopt as many as three or four children who may have lost their parents in the storm.

"A. C. and Our Home 1926 Storm"
(Granny's Photo Album)

Hurricanes are like mosquitoes. They blow in, they blow out, and they bite once in a while. On an average, they pass by Charlotte County every three years, and they directly hit every eleven years.

In the wake of the hurricane, on October 20, Granddaddy's father, Joseph J., died at age 60 in a Ft. Myers hospital after having a stroke. He was the first of many Frizzells to be buried in a family plot in the Charlotte Harbor Cemetery. The cemetery had been established in 1879, and it became the final resting place for many local pioneers and noteworthy leaders.

Johnnie [Granddaddy's brother],
Blanche and Joseph J. Frizzell [Granddaddy's parents]
(Probably the last photo taken of Joe).

The hurricane in September and the death of his father in October may have slowed Granddaddy, but by November, he was full steam ahead toward a new enterprise. With so many turpentine operations in the area, the sawmill business was a natural next step for him.

> November 30, 1926, **WANTED**
> "SAW MILL WANTED – Party with small saw mill to cut four to six million feet down timber. Only one-fourth mile haul to railroad.
> A. C. Frizzell, Murdock, Fla."

He first started buying land from big turpentine companies, after they had killed the pine trees on it by bleeding them for turpentine for three or four years. Real estate taxes made the once lucrative land a liability, and so he bought it for as little as fifty cents an acre.

Then with never ending patches of dead trees, he bought a small, portable sawmill, and he hired workers and leased convicts to cut the dead trees into lumber. They moved the sawmill from one patch of dead trees to the next.

"Sawmill"
(Granny's Photo Album).

"Saw Dust"
(Granny's Photo Album).

After each move, Granddaddy's sawmill left behind a landscape of stumps and palmettos. Stumps are heavy with resin, and so Granddaddy made a deal with Hercules Powder Company in Jacksonville for pine tar.

He then had his workers remove the stumps with an old automobile converted into a tractor and process the stumps into pine tar. They would dig a big hole in the ground, line it with sheet metal, and pile in the stumps. They set the stumps afire and covered them with sand taken from the hole in the ground. After the stumps smoldered for three days and nights, they began oozing pine tar, and a pipe carried the pine tar to an old bathtub. From the bathtub, the workers ladled the pine tar into barrels that Granddaddy shipped by rail to the Hercules Powder Company. There, it was processed into 117 products, which included gunpowder, paint thinner, and flavoring for lime sherbert. [10]

The stumps soon proved more profitable than lumber, and so Granddaddy bought one of the first bulldozers in the area. His bulldozer left behind a bare landscape speckled with palmettos, which catapulted him to the next phase in his illustrious career. The federal government was paying farmers to improve their soil, and so Granddaddy had his workers scrape off the palmettos, disk the ground, and plant Bahia grass for pasture.

He then added cattle to his stock-in-trade, at the same time expanding his timber operations to include the sale of charcoal, which was made from the wood of cut trees by burning it in pits, and the sale of rocks and cross ties to the railroad. He sold hearts of palm, which was cut from the cabbage palm (Florida's state tree) by workers who would climb a tree and carve out its heart, leaving behind a tree that had died in order to provide enough swamp cabbage for one southern barbecue. He later sold and shipped cabbage palms to a broom factory in Georgia.

At the same time that Granddaddy was setting up his sawmill operation in Murdock, a new neighbor was moving in thirty-five miles to the north. The Ringling Brothers and Barnum and Bailey Circus was establishing its winter quarters in Sarasota. At that time, John Ringling (middle of below photo) was the fifth wealthiest man in the U. S., and he and one of his brothers bought approximately 67,000 acres of what is now Sarasota. Granddaddy would later buy about 35,000 of those acres from them.

Ringling brothers circus poster. 1897.
Black & white photograph, 8 x 10 in. State Archives of Florida, Florida Memory.
<https://www.floridamemory.com/items/show/7908>
accessed 3 October 2018.

> July 24, 1927
> FOR SALE, Muscovy ducks, $2.50 each.
> Mrs. A. C. Frizzell, Murdock, Fla.

In August 1927, Granddaddy, then age 37, and Granny, age 56, applied to adopt a boy from The Children's Home of Hillsborough County in Tampa.

The home sent Recommendation Blanks to their references, including one to J. H. Lipscomb, the sheriff of Charlotte County. On the form, he stated that he had known Granddaddy and Granny for ten years, their property was worth more than $50,000 (over $500,000 today), and their fitness for the responsibility of training a child was "exceedingly good."

The Children's Home at 3302 Florida Ave. in 1927
The Burgett Brothers
"Courtesy, Tampa-Hillsborough County Public Library System."
http://digitalcollections.hcplc.org/digital/collection/p15391coll1/id/2813/rec/21, (accessed Feb. 7, 2018).

The form asked two questions about the husband that it did not ask about the wife. The first asked his occupation. In that blank, the sheriff answered, "Merchant." The second husband-only question asked, "Does he use liquor?" The sheriff answered, "No," with no mention of the bottle of liquor that Granddaddy drank every night, and everybody in town knew it. The sheriff also overstated Granddaddy's age by eight years, perhaps to minimize the twenty-year difference between his age and Granny's.

Mrs. Hiram Hart, Granny's dear friend in Tampa, sent a recommendation letter to the home. In it, she wrote, "I think it would be quite impossible for you to place any child in more loving hands than Mrs. Frizzel[l]." She ended her letter, "... the little boy would have ... an excellent future before him."

In December, The Children's Home placed two boys in the care of Granddaddy and Granny. They were brothers, age 6 and 4.

In that same month, Aunt Lula gave birth at the boarding house to a baby girl named Marijo. Soon after the birth, Aunt Lula, Uncle Tilley, and Marijo moved to Punta Gorda. Granddaddy had helped Uncle Tilley take over the Standard Oil agency there, and in 1928, Uncle Tilley built a stucco and brick Standard Oil Station on the corner of Highway 41 and Marion Avenue, now a flower shop.

Through the years, Granddaddy helped many of his family and friends get started with businesses. He was the big daddy of the community, and he did not concern himself with repayment. When he died, the outstanding total was hundreds of thousands of dollars, all of which he forgave.

On January 5, 1928, Granddaddy and Granny completed an adoption application for the Children's Home. In it, Granddaddy wrote that they would legally adopt the two boys at the end of a three-month trial period. He wrote that their object in taking a child was "to have a child to love and raise as our own."

At some point during the trial period, Granddaddy and Granny filed court proceedings in Charlotte County to legally adopt the two boys, but their biological mother's circumstances had changed, and she wanted them back. After a court battle in Tampa that lasted a month, the biological mother won custody of her two sons, who were by her first husband. She had reconciled her second marriage, was no longer destitute as a single mother, and proved to the judge that she and her husband were willing and able to care for the children. Because the biological father had not signed the document transferring legal guardianship to The Children's Home, the judge ruled in her favor. She declared that it was her happiest day, while Granny cried that it was her saddest.[11]

The U. S. census reveals that in 1930, the mother and her husband were living together with the two boys in Belle Glade. The older boy would grow up to be principal of a Marion County middle school.

That same month after Granddaddy and Granny lost custody of the two boys after having them for five months, the Children's Home placed another boy in their care for a three-month trial period. He was a red-haired, blue-eyed, freckle-faced four-year-old, who had been left at the home the year before. His mother had signed a form appointing the Children's Home guardian of her son and waiving all rights as his natural guardian.

This time, Granddaddy and Granny successfully adopted a son, my father Arthur Paul Frizzell.

Daddy on a car and beside the Texaco gas pumps at the Mercantile, with the hotel in the background across Highway 41.

The above photo is probably the last photo of the Murdock hotel before it blew away forever. Only a few months later, on September 16, 1928, Florida's deadliest hurricane relentlessly swept across the state from Palm Beach westward with 140-mile-per-hour winds that made it the fifth most intense Atlantic storm ever. It destroyed almost everything in its path, hitting the Lake Okeechobee area the worst.

Lake Okeechobee (the Seminole word for *big water)* is centrally located in the southern half of Florida's peninsula north of the Everglades and about thirty miles east of the Charlotte County line. The shallow lake measures slightly less than twenty-five miles by thirty-five miles, for a total of approximately 700 square miles, almost as big as Charlotte County.

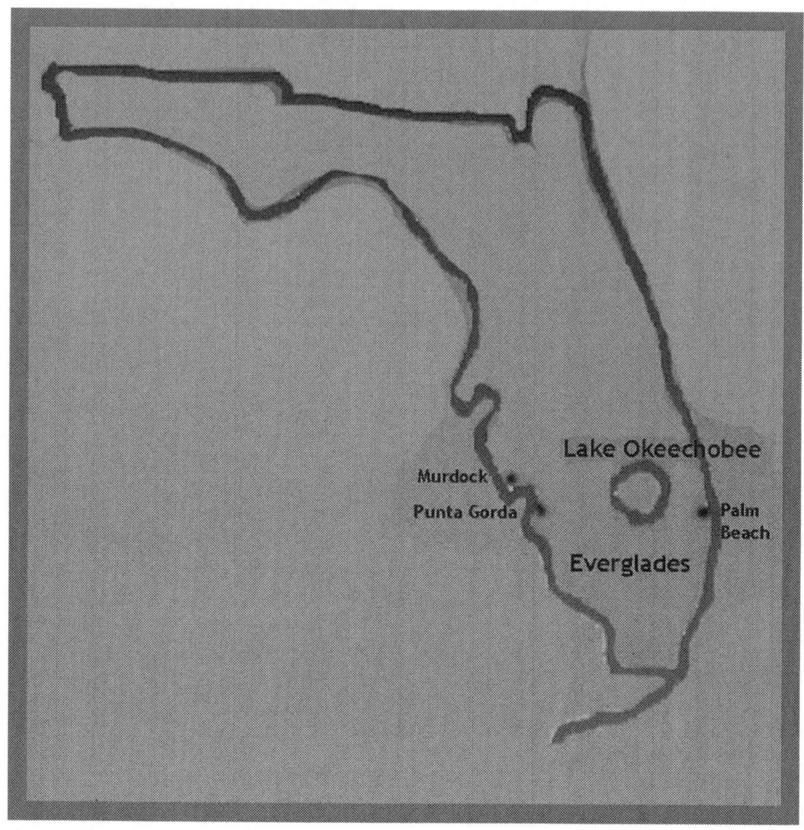

Between Lake Okeechobee and the Everglades, for over a century now, thousands of people have been working in fields that boast some of the richest soil in the world. The fields produce sugarcane, beans, tomatoes, cabbage, potatoes, and cucumbers, all of which thrive in two to thirty inches of lowland black muck.

When the Okeechobee Hurricane hit there and destroyed a four-foot-high dike around the lake, the fields flooded, and the workers faced an unimaginable terror before their untimely deaths. The rushing lake water rose an inch a minute until it reached its peak at twenty feet high. It stretched seventy-five miles by six miles wide and stayed high for two or three weeks.

The Red Cross estimated that there were 1,836 fatalities, of which twenty-six were in Palm Beach and the remainder in the Lake

Okeechobee area. 1,836 was the official count used by the National Weather Service for years and the exact official count for Hurricane Katrina. In 2003, however, Okeechobee's figure was revised to over 2,500, and then in 2009 to over 4,000, with 75% being black migrant workers.

The revised toll of 4,000 may still be an underestimate. There were so many dead bodies that floated into the saw grass of the Everglades, never to be found, and there were so many migrant workers and their families that no one knew were there, especially the ones from foreign countries, such as the Bahamas. Even those who were known to be missing could not be identified by survivors, because they knew most of them only by nicknames.

The Okeechobee Hurricane of 1928 was the second deadliest natural disaster in the history of the United States; the Galveston Hurricane of 1900 was the first, killing between 10,000 and 12,000 on the island.

Although there were no fatalities in Charlotte County from the hurricane, there was considerable property damage. In Punta Gorda, it flooded the streets, blew roofs off buildings, and sank boats; in Murdock, it destroyed buildings, among them the hotel and the Mercantile.

From the destroyed buildings, Granddaddy salvaged enough lumber to build four small houses for his employees, and he built a new concrete block Mercantile with an office for himself in one corner and a post office in another. He built it on some property he owned on the north side of Highway 41 at the intersection with Highway 776.

Granddaddy also salvaged lumber from buildings in the McCall area. Before the hurricane hit, he had started buying property there. McCall was another small railroad town that popped up about the same time as Ona, Vandolah, and Murdock. It was located across the Myakka River from El Jobean at the curve in the road. It was named for C. B. McCall, who was superintendent of the C. H. & N.

The town had developed around a turpentine camp and a sawmill. In 1905, the C. H. & N. built a two-story depot there called the Section Station, and in 1909, residents built a one-room school and two churches of different denominations. In that same year, John Densten built a store with a post office, and he served as postmaster.

Over ten years later, his future daughter-in-law, Madge Kinney, would serve as El Jobean's first postmistress, and she would hold that position for more than forty years. She once compared the size of the El Jobean post office to that of an outhouse. Trains did not stop there, but workmen would deliver bags of mail by throwing them from the train to the ground and pick them up by reaching down and snatching them from the ground.

Before Joel Bean built the post office, Madge had lived and worked there for three or four years as a dressmaker and letter carrier. Letter carrying meant that she rowed a boat a half mile across the Myakka River and then walked another half mile to John Densten's post office to pick up the mail. Neither rain nor heat nor snakes nor alligators nor mosquitoes stayed this courier from her appointed round.

Madge Densten
at the El Jobean Post Office Service Window after her Retirement.
Madge Kinney Densten, Southland Postmaster ::
Charlotte Harbor Area Historical Society and U.S. Cleveland,
http://ccflhistory.contentdm.oclc.org/cdm/ref/collection/p15007coll1/id/3913,
(accessed December 23, 2018).

The train stopped in McCall for about twenty years, and so its settlers used the railroad to ship wild hogs caught in the woods and watermelons grown on their farms, but in 1928, McCall became a nonstop station. At that point, Granddaddy started buying property there, and between 1928 and 1934, he demolished most of the homes in the vicinity. One McCall Section House, built in 1905, did survive, and it was the last remaining structure associated with the railroad, when it burned in 2004.[12]

Now, nothing remains of McCall at the intersection of Highways 771 and 776. It is one of Charlotte County's "Lost Towns."

In addition to buying the McCall property in 1928, Granddaddy expanded his sawmill operations by leasing land for timber. He signed eight timber contracts for a total of 780 acres, most of them for a period of eighteen months and all with similar terms: a down payment with installment payments due as he cut the timber. Then in 1929, he signed another contract for fifteen months on forty acres, and in 1930, he signed one for 305 acres east of Punta Gorda, about where the airport is today, for a total of over 1,100 acres leased for timber.

In March, 1929, he stocked his new Mercantile. For $2,500 cash plus a debt assumption in the amount of $200 for a Frigidaire cabinet and $77 for a cash register, he bought all the "goods, ware and merchandise, stock and fixtures, oils and gas, and all personal property of any nature now in or on the property known as Solana Service Station." Solana is an area east of Punta Gorda.

The new Mercantile (photo taken years later in 1947).

The year 1929 would end the booming, roaring twenties with the stock market crash and the beginning of the Great Depression that lasted at least a decade. October 29 (Black Tuesday) marked the day that stock market investors lost billions, and those who had saved their money in banks lost even more.

For many, the financial loss was too great to bear. Many investors jumped from New York City skyscraper windows, and even more asphyxiated themselves with gas, while others shot or poisoned themselves. They were devastated; big businesses were devastated, too, and they closed their doors to workers. The unemployment rate soared to 25% in the U. S. and as high as 33% in other countries.

While doors were closing throughout the world, yet another door of opportunity was opening for Granddaddy and Granny. They had wisely invested their money in land, and Granny, because she did not trust banks, had stashed their cash in her mattress, according to family lore, rather than in one of the three banks in Punta Gorda that had sadly closed in 1929.

It was during the depression years, while the rest of the world was hungry, that Granddaddy and Granny built an empire. They built it by buying land for delinquent taxes that had not been paid for two years. On the outside steps of the new courthouse in Punta Gorda, Granddaddy bought thousands of acres for 20 to 30 cents each, including most of Joel Bean's 4,000 acres of land in El Jobean.

Charlotte County courthouse - Punta Gorda, Florida. 1926.
Black & white photoprint, 8 x 10 in. State Archives of Florida, Florida Memory. <https://www.floridamemory.com/items/show/27551>, (accessed 26 April 2018).

Joel Bean had gone bankrupt. A farming project he had started the year before ended, he could not pay the taxes on his El Jobean land, and he held bad promissory notes to mortgaged properties.

Rather than return to Boston in poverty, he stayed in Charlotte County and lived in his El Jobean hotel. He did not give up, and he joined forces with Granddaddy to sell land. Both of their names appeared on an advertisement for 17,000 acres of Florida land for sale "at depression prices" in the "most uniform climate in America."

> March 10, 1930, Tampa Tribune
> WANTED – Colored tie choppers, pay 30c per tie, plenty of pine timber. Good place to live.
> Roy Frizzell, Punta Gorda, Fla.

Seaboard Air Line Railway employees laying track [cross ties] ... 1902.
Black & white photoprint, 5 x 7 in. State Archives of Florida, Florida Memory.
<https://www.floridamemory.com/items/show/25713>, (accessed 27 April 2018).

By 1930 when he placed the above ad, Granddaddy's youngest brother, Roy, was living in Solana on the east side of Punta Gorda. He was twenty-three years old, and he managed a grocery store there. Two years before, he had married Sarah Lee Thompson, and a year later, they had a son named William. William would grow up to be a well-known architect in Southwest Florida. He designed over 1,000 buildings around Florida, among them schools and libraries for many South Florida towns.

At the time of Uncle Roy's ad for "colored tie choppers," a man named John William Whaley was already at work chopping railroad cross ties for Granddaddy. He and his wife Bertha had migrated to Florida from Albany, Georgia, with their daughter, Susie. After the family moved through several communities to the Venice area, Susie met and married a young preacher named Frank Allen from Tallahassee. Then sometime in 1929, they all four moved to Murdock, where John and Frank went to work for Granddaddy. John contracted to cut and finish railroad cross ties. After John cut the ties, Frank loaded them into a truck and hauled them through the woods to the railroad station.

In 1932, Granddaddy would close his Murdock sawmill and open one near Immokalee, about 80 miles southeast of Murdock. John Whaley was among those workers who moved themselves and their families from Murdock to Immokalee to continue working for Granddaddy.

In Immokalee, Frank did most anything, but he worked primarily as a mechanic. He did all of the sawmill maintenance and a lot of the truck maintenance. When he was not working, he was preaching.

Shortly after they had first arrived in Murdock, Frank and Susie had a son named John Henry Allen. John Henry grew up and worked for Granddaddy, too, in the 1940's. He helped cut cabbage palms and prepare them for shipment to a broom factory in Georgia. John Henry was the third generation in his family to work for Granddaddy. His grandfather, John Whaley, would work for Granddaddy for over 20 years, until the day that he died in 1952.

On August 4, 1994, when John Henry was 64 years old, Micheāl Bergstrom interviewed him for an article in the *Sarasota Herald-Tribune*. He asked him what it was like for the blacks who worked for Granddaddy.

John Henry replied, "They got along. It was just a job. There was nothing exciting about it. And they just did what they had to do to make a living. All I can say is that when I worked for Frizzell he paid me what he said he was going to pay me and that was that.

"The times dictate how people treat people in a lot of instances. And that's the way it was back then. There was a lot of prejudice. But Frizzell was not as bad as others that I'd had contact with.

"He kept a lot of black folks working. I think he had more blacks working for him than anybody. And probably the reason they stayed with him was that he was as fair as he could be at that time. Of course, back then it was hard for black people to find any kind of work, and most of them were unemployed." [13]

Sometime around 1950, John Henry joined the Air Force. He served for four years, which included a tour in Korea.

When he returned to civilian life, he became one of Punta Gorda's most prominent citizens. According to a Proclamation by the city of Punta Gorda, he worked "tirelessly for justice and equality" and spent "a lifetime for the betterment of all residents of his community."

He "was instrumental in reorganizing the dormant NAACP in Charlotte County, serving as its President for ten years," and he joined other black activists to integrate Charlotte High School in Punta Gorda in 1965. Five out of eighteen black students were admitted that year. The others still had to ride a bus twenty-five miles to Ft. Myers.

On April 26, 2011, John Henry Allen died at the age of 81, and within a month, the mayor of the City of Punta Gorda signed a Proclamation to honor his memory. City Councilmen proclaimed May 21, 2011, John Henry Allen Day, and they had a ceremony in the Changing Exhibit Room in the Blanchard House Museum of African American History and Culture of Charlotte County. They dedicated the room to him and renamed it the John H. Allen Gallery.

The Proclamation stated that "his community service had been recognized by: his appointment to the Bicentennial Steering Committee by former Lt. Governor Tom Adams; a commendation by State Representative Vernon Peeples; an award for Activism in Civil Rights from the Women's Missionary Society of the 11th Episcopal District of Florida; and the Genesis Award for Creative Citizenship from the University Club of Charlotte County."

April 27, 1930, **Livestock**:
FOR SALE 3 female and 5 male full-blooded German police puppies: females, $5; males, $10.
Mrs. A. C. Frizzell, P. O. Box 56, Murdock, Fla.

PROCLAMATION

City of Punta Gorda, Florida

WHEREAS, the Blanchard House Museum is dedicated to educating the residents of Charlotte County and visitors to the rich history, culture and contributions of African Americans in our County; and

WHEREAS, the *Changing Exhibit Room* will be renamed as the *John H. Allen Gallery* to honor and celebrate the devotion and commitment of this dedicated citizen; and

WHEREAS, John Henry Allen, born in Murdock, spent a lifetime for the betterment of all the residents of his community; and

WHEREAS, John Allen served in the Air Force for four years, which included a tour in Korea, after which he returned to Punta Gorda to work tirelessly for justice and equality; and

WHEREAS, John Allen was instrumental in reorganizing the dormant NAACP in Charlotte County, serving as its President for ten years; and

WHEREAS, John Allen's community service has been recognized by his appointment to the Bicentennial Steering Committee by former Lt. Governor Tom Adams, a commendation by State Representative Vernon Peeples, an award for Activism in Civil Rights from the Women's Missionary Society of the 11th Episcopal District of Florida and the Genesis Award for Creative Citizenship from the University Club of Charlotte County; and

WHEREAS, it is fitting and just that his memory be honored by the dedication of the *John H. Allen Gallery;*

NOW, THEREFORE, The City Council of the City of Punta Gorda, Florida does hereby proclaim May 21, 2011 as

JOHN HENRY ALLEN DAY

and urges all residents to attend the dedication of the *John H. Allen Gallery* in his honor.

PASSED AND DULY ADOPTED in regular session this 18th day of May, 2011.

CITY OF PUNTA GORDA, FLORIDA

ATTEST:

Harvey Goldberg, Mayor

Sue Foster, City Clerk

In the summer of 1930, Jack and Joyce Hindman moved to Murdock. They were the sons of Granddaddy's sister, Lavona, and her husband, Richard, who owned a filling station in Gadsden. Jack was only seven at the time, and he lived with his Grandma Blanche in the boarding house. Joyce was ten and able to help Granny in the Mercantile. He hitchhiked to school in Punta Gorda and worked in the Mercantile every afternoon. In his spare time, he went hunting with a bird dog for wild turkey and quail. He lived in the back of the Mercantile with Uncle Forney, who also worked in the Mercantile.

Uncle Forney in front of the Mercantile.

Uncle Forney had divorced in 1926, after moving with his wife and daughter from Gadsden to Rome, Georgia, where his mother-in-law lived, and then to Atlanta. In Gadsden, he held various positions with the railroad; in Rome, he worked as a waiter in a restaurant; and in Atlanta, he worked in sales and management for a grocery store chain.

Now, he was living and working in Murdock with most of his family nearby. His mother Blanche and his brother Johnnie were still living in the boarding house across the road, and Johnnie worked nearby as a state road laborer. His brother A. C. lived down the road with his family, and his brother, Roy, and his sister, Lula, were living in Punta Gorda with their families. Only two sisters, Vona and Lizzie, were missing, and they were both in Alabama.

The next spring on March 25, 1931, tragedy struck at Granddaddy's favorite watering hole, the Acline Wine Place. In the late afternoon before the evening customers arrived, a big black man knocked on the door and wanted to have a drink inside, instead of at the window out back that Mack had reserved for his black customers.

Since no white folks were there to see a twist in his hospitality, Mack let him in and inquired, "What is it that you would like?"

The man said, "All of your cash," and aimed a gun at Mack.

Mack did not give him the cash, but pulled a pistol out instead; the bandit quickly opened fire, and plugged poor Mack six times with lead.

Ma screamed.

The bandit turned and ran across the floor; Mack grabbed a shotgun from behind the door. He blew off the bandit's head, and they both fell over dead.

The Acline Wine Place would then be known as Ma's Place.

Nearly three years after poor Mack was killed, the revenue agents from Jacksonville were headed Ma's way to investigate, when at last the Volstead Act was repealed. But when Ma became legitimate, the business was no longer fun for her, and so she sold her famous place and disappeared without a trace.[14]

Six months later, federal prohibition agents were on the warpath making arrests and seizing moonshine stills. They arrested one man with a sack of sugar on his back at a still two miles northwest of Murdock. It was one of many arrests made at stills in the Murdock woods throughout the years. Another worthy of mention occurred back in 1919, when a man was arrested there and thrown in the "county bastile" for manufacturing moonshine with a lard can.

"Mr. & Mrs. AC Frizzell"
(Granny's Photo Album).

CATTLE

He was the first cattleman in Southwest Florida to import Brahmans.

The year 1931 would be the year when Granddaddy's land became known as a cattle ranch. Although he had been dealing with cattle for about ten years, he said, "it wasn't until 1931 that I really started getting into the cattle business."[1]

He had bought a few cattle beginning in the early 1920's, but most of his cattle at that time were the wild, unbranded ones that were descendants of those left behind by the Spaniards in the 1500s, and they freely roamed the land. His workers rounded them up for him.

Local cowmen had been rounding up wild cattle for decades and shipping them to Cuba, where there was a shortage as a result of the Spanish-American War that had ended in 1898. The cowmen would drive herds of as much as 1,000 head through the streets of Punta Gorda to a loading dock there, or they would drive them through the swampy woods to Cattle Dock Point across from El Jobean on the west side of the Myakka River.

In 1931, Granddaddy added the cattle business to his other businesses, and he conducted them all from his small, cluttered office in a corner of the Mercantile, where he sat in an over-sized, cushioned chair at a roll-top desk. There, he would meet with other notable Florida cattlemen, such as the Vanderbilts and the Lykes brothers. The seven Lykes brothers were the largest landowners in Florida, the ninth largest in the U. S., and the wealthiest family in the Tampa Bay area. Granddaddy's youth, ambition, hard work, long hours, and shrewdness would establish him as one of the most successful businessmen in the state of Florida.

> November 22, 1931, **LIVESTOCK**
> FOR SALE – Four good farm mules, $85 each.
> A. C. Frizzell, Murdock, Fla.
>
> January 2, 1932, **LIVESTOCK**
> FOR SALE -- Two good farm mules, $65 each.
> P. O. Box 56, Murdock, Fla.
>
> January 3, 1932
> WANTED -- Good second-hand one-horse wagon.
> P. O. Box 56, Murdock, Fla.

At the same time that Granddaddy was conducting business in his office in the Mercantile, his workers were spending their hard-earned pay there. They either charged their purchases to an account that would be deducted from their earnings, or they paid with coins that Granddaddy had minted.

The coins that he minted were stamped out of babbitt metal, an alloy normally used for bearings. According to Trantow, the dollar, the five- and the 25-cent coins were made from brass; the ten-cent coins were made from aluminum. The coins were good only "in merchandise" at the Mercantile, but redeemable for cash at the end of each month.

The payment of earnings with babbitt coins to be used for shopping at the company store was a common practice by U. S. lumber companies at the time. Most of them were located so remotely that towns with banks and shopping were not easily accessible.

Frizzell Lumber Company babbitt coins from my brother Steve's collection.

While many folks called Granddaddy *Mr. A. C.* or *Mr. Murdock,* his workers sometimes called him *Babbitt Dad,* but *Babbitt Dad* did not often circulate babbitt coins. At the end of each week, he deducted from his workers' pay such items as: Doctor, Rent, Mercantile Account, and S. S. Tax. He also deducted jail bail plus ten percent interest. Rarely was there a Balance Paid.

Nº 4086

Immokalee, Fla., ...194....

Name ....

Dept. .... Amount $........................

Deduct: Dr. $........................

Rent $........................

Acct. $........................

S. S. Tax $........................ Total $........................

Balance Paid $........................

FRIZZELL LUMBER CO., INC.

By...

Not Transferable

The "Rent" deduction was for the houses that Granddaddy built for his workers and their families. Across from the new train depot, he eventually built a total of about a dozen small, white frame houses.

Later, he would build a church/school, too, but, in the beginning, there was no building, although there was a church. The Beulah Baptist Church was "constituted" in Murdock in 1919 by the National Baptist Convention. The NBC had formed in 1895 in order to unify nearly two million former slaves who attended Baptist churches in eleven states. After the church was "constituted," from 1920 to 1923, services were held in private homes; then, from 1923 to 1938, they were held in a building; and in 1938, Granddaddy built a new building to be used for both church and school.[2]

The new building, located next to the houses, was an "unpainted, rectangular, Meeting-hall type, frame building."[3] It was tall and narrow with wooden shutters on the windows and a fishing pond in the back.[4]

During the week, the building served as a one-teacher school. The teacher used a "primer book" and was paid $55 per month to teach about fifteen children from the ages of six to fourteen.[5] A primer was a small first book for teaching children to read.

On their way to school, the young girls often stopped at one of the lady's houses for sewing or quilting sessions, where patterns and recipes were exchanged. The ladies would make dresses for them with bleached sugar sacks that they decorated with colored bias tape.[6]

Then after school, the girls would join the boys to pick berries for pies and guavas for jelly.

Once in a while, both the girls and the boys would miss school, when they went with their fathers on ten-day raccoon hunts in Big Slough. Their fathers would take time off from the ranch to trap and skin raccoons, and then sell the hides to a man from Arcadia. With the real money that they made, they were able to take their families on shopping sprees in Punta Gorda.[7]

But they lived off the land as much as they could. They ate lots of beef from the ranch. Some of them had relatives who were fishermen and would bring them salted mullet to eat in the off season. They ate chickens that first entertained them when they ran from house to house with their heads chopped off. It was fun to congregate on the front stoop of one of the houses and laugh at the headless chickens.

In the mornings at sunup, when the men mounted their horses and rode through the front gate of the Quarters on their way to work, they did so with great pride. They were skilled at what they did, and they were among a rare breed of Florida cowboys who looked down their noses at the western cowboy. In their minds, the word *cowboy* had a negative connotation, and they preferred to be called *cowhunter, cowpuncher,* or *cracker cowboy.*

Florida cowboys distinguished themselves from western cowboys by using bullwhips, instead of lassos, to herd or capture cattle. They were experts at cracking the whip, and their expertise gave birth to the native Floridian name *cracker.* They did not hit the cattle with the whip, but cracked it near their ears in order to control them. Dogs assisted in maintaining order.

Their gear and appearance also differed from the typical western cowboy. Because they did not need a saddle horn for lassos, many used the lightweight McClellan saddle, instead of the western saddle. Instead of western boots, they wore either brogans or boots that reached above the knees for snake protection. Instead of stereotype cowboy hats, they wore straw hats. [8]

Cracker Cowboy and *Arizona Cow-boy,* both by Frederic Remington.

When on the range and away from the chuck wagon, most Florida cowboys carried a small tin can with a wire bail tied to their saddles. They used the tin can to cook coffee, jerky, or salt pork over an open fire. If they had salt bacon, they cooked it on a stick over the coals. They cooked sweet potatoes, their favorite, in the ground under the fire.[9]

As for racial strife, it did not exist among Florida cowhands. Most of them enjoyed what they did, and so they put their differences aside, but at the end of the day, the whites went to where they lived, and the blacks went to where they lived, and it was always in a place called the Quarters.

> June 12, 1932:
> CROSS TIES for sale; 1500 good reject sap ties, 20 percent 6x8, 80 percent 7x8 and 7x6. Make offer. Address P. O. Box 56, Murdock, Fla.
> [Reject ties were those in danger of infection or possible decay, because they were not timely treated.]

In 1932, Granddaddy closed his sawmill operation in Murdock, and he opened two others. One was in Venus in the heart of Lykes brothers country, about eighteen miles south of Lake Placid and sixty miles east of Murdock. The other was ten miles south of Immokalee and about eighty miles southeast of Murdock. There, Granddaddy built a short railroad to move pine and cypress logs to the sawmill, and he planted a watermelon field. His workers named the place Arzell, a contraction of Granddaddy's name, Arthur Frizzell.

Arzell Sawmill.

In addition to those who moved from Murdock to Immokalee to work for Granddaddy, his cowhands who stayed in Murdock often went to Immokalee to help with the work, too. They rode their horses eighty miles on well-worn cattle tracks. After they loaded their saddlebags with coffee, lard, flour or meal, they hit the trail for three or four nights of sleeping under the stars. Along the way, they lived off the land, hunting various birds, which they cooked over an open fire. For drink, they dipped water from creeks with their straw hats.[10]

In Immokalee, Granddaddy hired Sammie King and his wife, Hattie. Sammie was a skilled cowhand and Hattie, a cook. He moved them both to the Quarters in Murdock, so that Sammie could train cowhands there and chauffeur Granddaddy. Hattie would later cook for Granddaddy and his family. They both would become a part of our family.

Sammie and Hattie King in front of Mercantile 1948.

In the fall of 1932 after Granddaddy opened Arzell Sawmill, Granny and Daddy moved there, but they returned to Murdock on weekends. In December, they moved back to Murdock.

Daddy had started his third grade of school in Immokalee, but would finish it back at the Charlotte Harbor Schoolhouse, where he had completed his first two grades. He had missed the first month of his first year there, but at the end of his second year, he received an Award of Honor for eight months of perfect attendance.

"Paul's 1st Grade Room," 1930
[in front of the Charlotte Harbor Schoolhouse,
Daddy back row, first on left] (Granny's Photo Album).

Daddy with a Calf.

In March 1933, Granny's son Lemuel returned to Murdock for a visit. He brought his wife, Alice, and stepson, Gerry, with him.

Lemuel had been living in Birmingham, where he was an industrial engineer for J. T. Sudduth & Company, a company that dealt in machinery, fences, and road builders.

In 1930, he was a roomer in the same boarding house as Alice Marion Foster. The two of them met there, and they married in 1931. Lemuel was 34, and Alice was 36.

Alice had been married twice before. The daughter of a sea captain, she had lived in many ports, and so taking off to Panama with her first husband, a reporter, was easy for her to do. After having a baby boy, Gerry, in Panama, she took off again, this time on a ship to New Orleans without her husband. Immediately after disembarking, she married a fellow passenger, who was a mechanic, and they later had a baby girl, Mary.

It appears that Lemuel and Alice returned to Birmingham after their visit in Murdock, but Alice's son, Gerry, then age 19, stayed behind.

A couple of months later, Granddaddy went to the hospital in Tampa for a gall bladder operation. Complications developed, and he stayed there for almost two months.

When Granddaddy first entered the hospital, Granny took Daddy to Wauchula to stay with Annabel, and she arranged for Daniel Child to work in the Mercantile and the post office. By this time, Uncle Forney was working at a store in Punta Gorda.

With Granddaddy in Tampa and Granny gone visiting him most of the time, the cat was away, and the boys of Murdock played. They gravitated to the Mercantile, and they transformed it into the social hub of Murdock.

Daniel wrote in his diary that Uncle Johnnie and Gerry practically lived in the store. They kicked off their boots, and they hung their hats there. They ate their lunches there. One day, Uncle Johnnie went cowhunting, but he took breaks at the store two or three times. Another day, even though Gerry was trying to pen a new heifer, he popped in and out all day long. Another day, Gerry moped around the store, "feeling abused when he got up late and found the cook Fanny King, colored, had been let out" during Granny's absence.

"Fannie the Cook" (Granny's Photo Album).

May 9, 1933, Daniel Child

BEER SOLD LEGALLY IN FLORIDA YESTERDAY

Tampa not enthusiastic.

CERVEZA TROPICAL (HABANA)

In Punta Gorda 25 cents bottle

In Arcadia 35 cents bottle

Payday at the Seaboard Airline Railway was always a busy day at the Mercantile, but one particular day in May, it was a downright party, according to Daniel. It started in the morning, when Gerry and a young bakery man set up an ice cream and cake booth. Gerry contributed ice cream cups, and the bakery man some five-cent cakes. Then, Uncle Johnnie borrowed $100 cash from Uncle Tilley, so he could cash paychecks and immediately be able to collect what the workers owed on their Mercantile accounts. Granny had hired Uncle Johnnie to work in the Mercantile and moved Daniel to the post office only.

Her new arrangement was unsuccessful, and a couple of weeks later, she stormed into the Mercantile a little before noon and soon had things "moving in a hurry." She called a couple of friends from Ona to replace Uncle Johnnie and Daniel. Daniel could still work outside and might be allowed to haul ties, but he was "let out." "Credit was tightened, greater production required of the colored force, and some were to be removed."

On July 1, Granddaddy finally returned home, and the next day, Gerry was in charge of the store and the post office. Granny's friends returned home to Ona.

About the time that Granddaddy fully recuperated, he drove one of two cars loaded with Murdock people to a singing convention forty miles away in Gardner, Florida, where Granny had once worked as station agent. Granddaddy drove his Lincoln with Granny, Daddy, and five others in it, while Uncle Johnnie drove his car with Grandma Blanche and five others.

> August 20, 1933, Daniel Child:
> The upstairs auditorium of the fine brick school building was packed. Just before lunch, the lady principal of the Gardner school welcomed us with a sentence or two. The welcome was responded to by a Mr. Brown who told briefly of the founding of the DeSoto Singing Convention, about 1896, by Thornhill, with only a few singers, where now there are many. Another man offered prayer. There were many specials and great congregational singing and great piano playing.
>
> The style of music was snappy with quick tempo and choruses of some difficulty. Only a few old time pieces were sung.
>
> Lunch was with Johnnie and Grandma [Blanche]. We had fried chicken, bread and biscuits, boiled eggs, custard pie, cake, jelly, and guavas that I brought.

Fall 1933 started with Granny hosting a pound party at the schoolhouse in September. A pound party is one to which each guest brings a pound of food. The food can be for just about any cause, such as a church pantry, a needy family, or for newlyweds. Daniel wrote that there was plenty of cake and pie and iced lemonade. About thirty-five were present, several from Punta Gorda.

Then in the month of October, Granny was back working in the post office, while Granddaddy's hogs were running wild all over the place. They were rooting up Daniel's yard, and one of them ate his white hen. The more Daniel complained to Granddaddy about them, the more they ran loose. He would chase them away, and they would return. In December, he was still chasing. It was a never ending battle that continued for years.

Also in October, Charlotte County held a special election regarding the upcoming repeal of the 18th amendment, which had mandated nationwide prohibition starting in January 1920. It would be the only amendment repealed from the constitution. Florida, however, was among two-thirds of the states that allowed each county to vote on whether to be wet or dry. Charlotte County voted wet.

By then, election day in Murdock had become quite a social affair. The ladies brought food and drink, and people congregated around the polling place. One lady brought boiled peanuts, another brought candy, and others brought sandwiches. One man furnished water for both the "wets" and the "drys" to drink. And the sheriff showed up with a lady on his arm.

Listed among the five "dry" voters were Grandma Blanche and Daniel Child; listed among the eleven "wet" voters were Granddaddy, Granny, and Joel Bean. Although Granny detested alcohol and had preached temperance, she was now standing by her man. In defense of their wet votes, Joel Bean proclaimed, "Liberty is the most precious gift that heaven has given men."

Not long after the election, Granddaddy formed a partnership with S. W. Sweat of Mulberry, Florida, to remove timber on 1,280 acres of Sweat's land for two years, and they would split all the expenses and profits. Each partner could not do anything without the written consent of the other. The partnership only lasted seven months, at which time Granddaddy ended it. In exchange for Granddaddy's interest in the business, Sweat gave him 30,000 feet of flooring, ceiling, and framing, while Sweat was allowed to use Granddaddy's sawmill and equipment until the timber was exhausted and return it to him in good repair. Granddaddy also rented him four mules for $12 per month until the timber was cut.

Also in early November, Granddaddy bought over 7,000 acres of land, most of it along Highway 41 south of Punta Gorda in the vicinity of the Acline Wine Place, but big chunks on Jones Loop Road and Burnt Store Road, plus over thirty lots in Punta Gorda. The purchase was all of the Charlotte County holdings of a widow from Sarasota County.

At the end of the month, seventeen Murdock Baptists piled into a couple of cars again, with eight including Granny in her Lincoln, and they took off to Punta Gorda for the 44th anniversary meeting and homecoming for the Punta Gorda Baptist Church. They enjoyed music, visiting, and a splendid dinner at the tourist camp beside the old Charlotte Bridge. Food included fish, meats, salads, fruit, honey, cakes, pies, pickles, cheese, bread, sandwiches, coffee, jelly, and plenty of ice water.

A month later at a church meeting on New Year's Eve, Granny announced that the Mercantile was going to sell beer and asked if that would disqualify her as a Sunday School teacher. The news caused quite a ruckus and many "private consultations," before she resigned from all of her church positions a week later. Her positions included: secretary-treasurer, Sunday School teacher, and leader of the Women's Missionary Union.

January 16, 1934, Daniel Child
FRIZZELL DIPPING VAT REBUILT TODAY

In 1933, Charlotte County had announced that animal dipping inspections would begin there in 1934, in an effort to enforce a law passed by the state legislature ten years before in 1923. As indicated by Daniel Child's above diary entry, Granddaddy prepared for an inspection.

According to the Florida Department of Environmental Protection (FDEP), from 1906 through the 1950s, "approximately 3,200 cattle dip vats were constructed in rural areas of Florida." The vats were "filled with an arsenic solution for the control and eradication of the cattle fever tick. Other pesticides such as DDT were also widely used. By

State law, all cattle, horses, mules, goats, and other susceptible animals were required to be dipped every 14 days."

As of June 30, 2015, the FDEP continues an ongoing effort to locate the vats. "The arsenic and other pesticides remaining at the site[s] may present an environmental or public health hazard."[11]

The Florida Livestock Board listed known cattle dip vats by county as they were put into operation. One such vat listed under Charlotte County was named Frizzell in 1934.

Mule in a Tick Eradication Vat
Black & white photonegative, 4 x 5 in. State Archives of Florida, *Florida Memory*, https://www.floridamemory.com/items/show/13112 (accessed April 27, 2018).

In June 1934, Gerry left Murdock and joined the Merchant Marine. A year and a half later, his name would appear on the crew list of a ship named the SS *Endicott* that arrived in New Orleans from Kobe,

Japan. It was owned by Lykes Brothers Steamship Company, and so Granddaddy had probably arranged the job for him through his close business associates the Lykes brothers. Their company was known for shipping cattle and lumber to ports all over the world.

In November, the big happening of 1934 took place. Almost a year after Granny resigned from her church positions after announcing that she would be selling beer in the Mercantile, she threw out the beer!

She wrote her dear friend Miss Lyda (Mrs. Hiram Hart) in Tampa:

> One thing I have intended to write you about for a long time but just wasnt well and didnt. We only kept beer in the store at Murdock three months, long enough to convince Mr. A. C. it was the wrong thing to do and made a bigger impression on both of my boys of the wrongness of beer or alcoholic beverage, than all the talking or advising I could have given them.

The beer removal may or may not have caused a feud with Granddaddy, but within a couple of weeks, Granny and Daddy moved back to Arzell. They would live there this time, except for a few months in 1935, for almost four years, with weekend visits to Murdock. In her absence, Uncle Forney would work in the store and take over as postmaster.

It was not long before Granddaddy took another of his giant steps forward. "I got my first Brahman cattle about 1935," he said.[12]

He was the first cattleman in Southwest Florida to import Brahmans. He traveled to Texas, and he bought a registered herd there. He filled two trains with the cattle, one for himself and one for the Lykes brothers ranch near Lake Okeechobee.

The Brahmans thrived in the Florida climate, and they produced quality beef. Granddaddy soon disposed of his scrawny scrub cattle, and he gradually built up his herd to 50,000 head.

Along the main roads, he fenced his land, but everywhere else, his cattle roamed freely, including on Cape Haze land that he leased that would later be owned by the Vanderbilts. That land was located between Granddaddy's land and the coast.

In the dead of summer with its oppressive heat and ruthless mosquitoes, Granddaddy's cattle would swim from Cape Haze across what is now the Intracoastal Waterway to Don Pedro Island. There, they walked across a narrow strip of land and waded into the Gulf of Mexico so deep that only their heads and horns were visible. Local fishermen stayed away from wherever Granddaddy's cattle were swimming. They did not want to tangle their nets with a herd of Granddaddy's hot Brahmans.

While Granddaddy's hot Brahmans were roaming freely over the land for miles around, sometimes on their way for a swim, they would occasionally stop for pleasure visits with mixed breeds that did not meet with Granddaddy's approval. His Brahmans were pure, and he wanted to keep them pure, or they were mixed, and he wanted to do his own mixing.

In 1935 in McCall, there was one bull, in particular, that Granddaddy did not want mixing with his herd, and so he sent his cowhands to castrate the bull. The bull was owned by a young black man by the name of Abe Nightingale, who lived in McCall with his 17-year-old wife, Mary. Abe tended an orange grove there and preached in the Holiness Church.

When Abe asked Granddaddy's cowhands what had happened to his bull, they explained, "Mr. A. C. told us to put the emasculators on him."

Abe immediately tracked down Granddaddy and approached him, at a time when and in a place where black men did not approach white men. Nobody knows what Abe said, but Granddaddy paid him for the bull and gave him a full-blooded Brahma.

In an interview with Micheal Bergstrom, Abe's wife, Mary, explained, "My husband was a good man, help anybody he could, but he didn't take no punches off nobody. Not off nobody."

Twenty years later, when Granddaddy sold his ranch, the sale included the land where Abe's church was situated, and the church was evicted. According to Mary, the church had been buying the building, but Granddaddy still owned it.[13]

In October 1935, Granny wrote to her friend Miss Lyda (Mrs. Hiram Hart) in Tampa that she had "a break down and was not able to do a thing for a year, he [Daddy] was my dependence for some one to do little things for me, and he did every thing willingly and lovingly, nothing he can do for his Mama is too hard or too much, what I would have done without him I dont know."

At the time of Granny's breakdown, Daddy was in the sixth grade, and he missed the first few months of school that year, but his grades for the balance of the year were mostly A's. He probably missed those months, because he was helping Granny.

When she first had the breakdown, Granny had gone to Tampa to see Dr. Blake, "but was not able to go anyehere else and couldnt do much talking, as my heart was ... in bad shape."

Shortly after Granny's breakdown, on November 3, Lemuel and Alice visited her, and they visited Alice's daughter Mary, who was then living in Sarasota and attending Ringling School of Art.

Back in Murdock, Granddaddy was expanding his cattle operation. Daniel wrote that in February of the following year, 1936, Granddaddy shipped 300 head of cattle on the train. The price was $32 per head (big steers). A few days later, he made another shipment, for a total of 581 head. At $32 per head, the total was $28,192 (roughly $300,000 today).

A month later, Daniel saw Granny in a car with Uncle Johnnie. "She looked very white and unwell, but was, in fact, so she said, ten pounds or more overweight. She had just been sick for nine days in the Ft. Myers Hospital," after spending only a few days in a new house Granddaddy had bought for her and Daddy on Highway 29 in Immokalee.

That summer in July, Uncle Johnnie and Uncle Forney traveled 400 miles from Murdock to Sycamore, a tiny town in South Georgia, both with the plan to get married. They were only gone for a couple of days, but Uncle Forney did get married, and Uncle Johnnie met his future bride and would marry six months later.

Uncle Johnnie's Sycamore wife, Aunt Nellie, told me that she was a mail order bride. She said that Uncle Johnnie had advertised for a bride, because there were so few women in Murdock.

On July 7, 1936, Uncle Forney, who had been divorced for ten years and was 48 years old, married Annie Freeman, age 39. In the July 12 issue of the Macon Telegraph: their marriage was solemnized at the Methodist Parsonage in Ashburn, two miles from Sycamore. Annie was from a prominent south Georgia family, and she was educated in Sycamore schools. Her "costume" at the wedding was "navy sheer crepe with accessories to match." Uncle Forney was described as a "prominent business man of Murdock." Their attendants were Uncle Johnnie and his future bride Nellie Viola Powers, also of Sycamore.

Annie returned to Murdock with Uncle Forney, and she lived with him at the Mercantile, where she also worked with him. Shortly after their return, Daniel saw Uncle Forney and congratulated him. A few days later, he met Annie. "She is rather tall, but looks quite fragile, small, soft hands. Didn't converse with her, but like her looks."

The next month when Granny was visiting in Murdock, Daniel approached her to sign a petition against slot machines. She told him that she let A. C. decide politics, and she declined to sign it, unless he did.

A couple of months later, Daniel wrote that Johnnie was "bad in his mind, again." Among other things, he had been appointed to the election board, but had failed to pay his poll tax.

In spite of Uncle Johnnie's failure to pay the poll tax, Murdock's polling place moved to the front porch of his house that year, and the event took wings. The voter turnout that year was heavy, but no one knows for sure if it was for the candidates or the lemon pie. While voters enjoyed coffee and lunch, Joel Bean passed out pie and campaigned for Roosevelt.

> November 15, 1936
> WANTED - Someone unfit for manual labor to file crosscut saws in logging woods.
> Frizzell Lumber Co., Immokalee, Fla.

In 1936, Granddaddy only made about four purchases. In addition to the house he had bought in Immokalee, he also bought the Immokalee Cash store. In April, he bought 640 acres in the Murdock area on the north side of the intersection of Highways 41 and 776 across the railroad track from the Mercantile. Eleven years later, Daddy would live there with his bride. Then in July, he bought three acres in the McCall area from his acquaintance of more than fifteen years, W. A. Lampp, a big property owner in Englewood.

The next year began with the marriage of Uncle Johnnie, then age 37, and Aunt Nellie, age 33, on January 2, 1937. They rang in the new year at the Baptist pastorium in Punta Gorda, where they were married by Reverend J. H. Sutley, who used to preach at Murdock. Attendants were Uncle Forney and his wife, Annie, who had married six months earlier.

Daniel was at the Mercantile when the wedding party returned from Punta Gorda to celebrate. Johnnie set up the cool drinks. Daniel's was "Cuba Cola, a new one."

Uncle Johnnie and Aunt Nellie settled in Uncle Johnnie's house on some property that Granddaddy had deeded him in the middle of a grapefruit grove behind the Mercantile.

> January 16, 1937, Daniel Child
> Mr. Joel Bean came soon after dinner and got 1-1/2 dozen grapefruit for some people (man and woman in big car). I asked them 18 cents for the fruit and the man gave me 20 cents (tho he had the pennies) and told me to "keep the change." They went on toward Punta Gorda.

On May 15, 1937, Granny wrote a letter from Arzell to her friend Miss Lyda.

> Dear Miss Lyda,
>
> No, I have not forgotten you, nor desaed to love you, Paul and I often talk of you and wish we could see you.
>
> We came down here with our saw mills two years ago last Dec. and have been here with the exception of weekend trips to Murdock every isnce.
>
> Paul [age 13] has done well in school, will finsih 7th. grade on the 28th. and he is so smart and such a comfort and help ... He is now his Daddy's right hand man, can drive any aitomobile or truck on the place,

and does so many things, today he is out in the woods helping to build a road, of course this road couldnt be build without him.

He wighs 102 and is 4 ft 10 inch high. strong as a young ox and every one says is a most splendid boy makes friends easily but doesnt take up with every one he sees, is really discriminating in his choice of friends.

His ambition now is to be an architect, he has all kinds of tools and is taking mechanical drawing through a correspondence course, and doing well. He build himself a tool house which while it is not an example of beauty or anything like that it is a pretty well designed and built house for a youngster mhe made it last year. He is busy all the time, says he gets enough play at school, of course really all his work is play as it is things all boys like to do.

We do not know how much longer we will be here, probably two years, we are now 8 miles south of Immokalee but will go to Immokalee to live in about two months will have this location cut out.

...

We havnt been to Tampa for more than two years, is why I havent seen you ... as my heart ... still is in bad shape but not as bad as it was then as have over a years rest I dont work now only just little things around the house that I am able to do when I feel like it.

If and when we come to Tampa we are going to see you for I want you to see my big boy. With love from us both.

[signed] Mrs. A. C. Frizzell

Telegraph Telephone Express and Post Office } IMMOKALEE, FLA.

Bank Reference: Punta Gorda State Bank, Punta Gorda, Fla.

Mills Located on A. C. L. Ry. ARZELL, FLA.

FRIZZELL LUMBER CO.

INCORPORATED

Manufacturers of

YELLOW PINE LUMBER

Rough and Dressed

Immokalee, Florida

5-15-37

Dear Miss Lyda,

No I have not forgotten you,nor desaed to love you,Paul and I often talk of you ,and wish we could see you. We came down here with our saw mills two years ago last Dec. and have been here with the exception of week end trips to Murdock every isnce. Paul has done well in school ,will finsih 7th.grade on the 28th. and he is so smart and such a comfort and help.Last Octo a year ago I had a break down and was not able to do a thing for a year, he was my dependence for some one to do little things for me,and he did wvery thing willingly and lovingly, nothing he can do for his Mama is too hard or

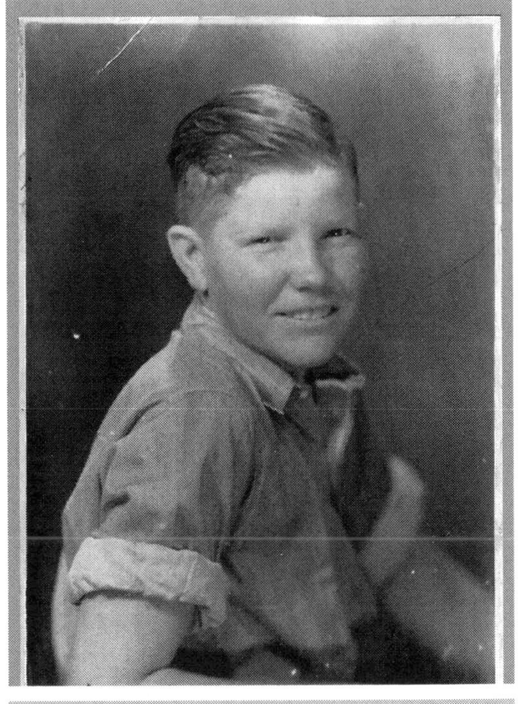

"My Big Boy"

Daddy completed the seventh grade in Immokalee with mostly A's and B's, and he was promoted to the eighth grade.

There is no record of him attending the eighth grade during the school term 1937-1938, when he should have. Perhaps, Granny kept him out of school to help her. If he did attend the eighth grade that year, he was not promoted, which is highly unlikely in view of his previous good grades throughout his school history, including throughout the ordeal of granny's breakdown.

> August 28, 1937, Daniel Child
> Got a late start getting ready to go to town and was out on road about 9 reading the Dailies (Tribune and News Press) when Mr. Collins came and stopped so I went to town with him and he brought back my cow feed and supplies. He also stopped at Standard Oil Headquarters and got kerosene and a message from Miss Lula for her mother at Murdock and a wire from A. C. away on a trip. Mr. Collins also set up Coca Cola at Red Wing's in Charlotte Harbor.

In Granny's absence, Red Wing's in Charlotte Harbor had become another of Granddaddy's favorite watering holes, but his main attraction there was Red Wing herself. According to family lore, his attraction was so strong that he bought her a house in Punta Gorda.

Also according to family lore, one night, he walked into the crowded bar and caught a cowboy trying to kiss Red Wing. She was struggling to free herself from him. Granddaddy pulled his gun from its holster and shot the man dead. Nobody in the bar saw it happen, or so they all said, and the incident died with the cowboy.

Did nobody really see it happen?

There is no record of when the shooting took place, but that summer of 1937, in what appears to be Granddaddy's first step toward a reconciliation, he took Granny on a trip of their lifetime. After they returned, Daniel rode with them in their car to Murdock from Punta Gorda one day, and they told him all about it. They had traveled 5,000 miles and visited nine states. Along the way, they went to New Mexico, Old Mexico, Pueblo in Colorado, the top of Pike's Peak, and Hot Springs, Arkansas.

Granny in Hot Springs, Arkansas.

November 21, 1937
BOOKKEEPER who can keep books for sawmill, make lumber invoices, check off employees and do other necessary office work. Apply in person, bringing letter of recommendation from former employer. No one over 48 years old need apply. Must be sober, honest, industrious and capable. Salary $125 per month. Frizzell Lumber Co., Immokalee, Fla.

Granddaddy rang in the new year 1938 by overturning his car on a dangerous curve on Highway 17 east of Punta Gorda. He spent several weeks in the St. Petersburg hospital and was still bandaged five weeks later, according to Daniel.

In late February, Granddaddy and Granny sold the house in Immokalee and then spent several months together in Ft. Myers. After that, Granny and Daddy moved back to Murdock.

That summer 1938, Granddaddy made the second of two sizable purchases in one year's time. He bought a parcel totaling more than 2,600 acres from Lenox Land & Improvement Co. of New York. The purchase included most of the land in the six touching sections highlighted in pink on the below map, a sizable chunk of what would later be Port Charlotte. The year before, he had bought over 10,000 acres in southeastern Sarasota County from the Lamar Land Company. He planned to fence the tract for cattle pasture.

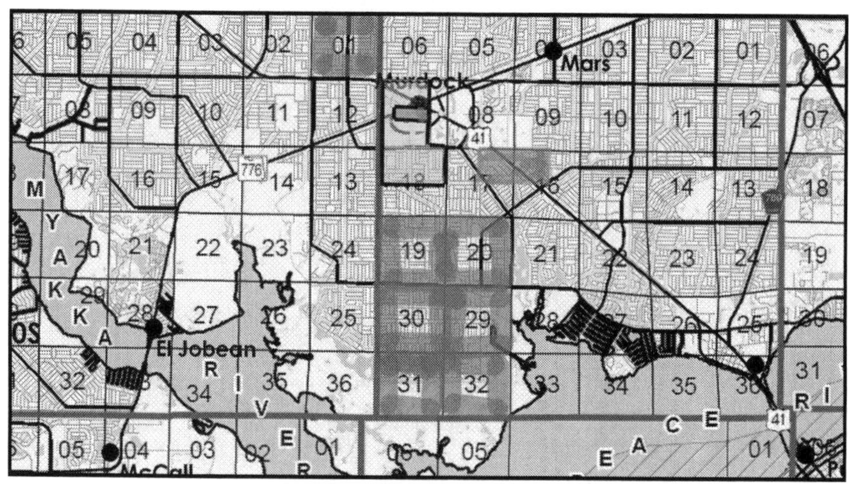

Frizzell Property 1938
(Charlotte County Section Map Transformed).

Also that summer, the Mercantile was robbed again. Early one morning in August, someone broke a glass window and stole about $65 worth of cigarettes, pocket knives, and shoes. Daniel wrote that a fingerprint was left on a piece of the broken glass. After that, Uncle Forney started sleeping inside the store with a high-power rifle.

In September, Grandma Blanche moved to a house on Harvey Street in Punta Gorda, where Joyce and Jack would live with her.

Joyce went to work for Uncle Tilley at the Standard Oil Agency. At night and on Saturdays after football practice, he drove a small pickup and delivered gasoline, kerosene, and diesel fuel to farmers.

The following month on Sunday, October 16, Granddaddy and Granny hosted an afternoon affair at their ranch. Family and friends from miles around, including Ft. Myers, enjoyed horseback riding and an exhibition by Granddaddy's cowboys followed by supper on the lawn in front of their home.[14]

A couple of months later on December 17, Aunt Nellie gave birth to Robert Preston, two years after she and Uncle Johnnie had married. Five years later, they would have another son Joseph "Buddy" Powers.

Shortly after they married, Uncle Johnnie had started working for Granddaddy on a new pasture improvement program that included the use of carpet grass. By the time Preston was born, Uncle Johnnie's work with carpet grass had expanded to helping Granddaddy experiment with different types of grasses for a wide variety of different soils on the ranch. They favored Pensacola Bahia, because of its drought resistance, but they tried pangola and torpedo grasses. Torpedo grass had been popular since the 1920's, because of its hardiness. It could survive drought, flooding, cattle grazing, and cattle stomping.

Now that Daddy was back living in Murdock, he was attending his eighth grade of school in Charlotte Harbor and after school, he helped Granddaddy and Uncle Johnnie with their grass projects; he also stirred up some rumors. He was 14 years old then, and everybody thought that he looked more like Granddaddy than he ever had. He had Granddaddy's blue eyes, but he had the red hair and freckles of a woman named Clara Mae Bell, who had lived next door. Granddaddy's kin gossiped that Daddy was Granddaddy's illegitimate son by her.

Clara Mae was originally from Mayo in North Florida, but the 1920 U. S. census shows her living with her father and his young wife next door to Granddaddy and Granny in Murdock. At that time, Granddaddy and Granny would have been living upstairs in the train depot beside the track, and so the Bells would have lived in a railroad section house beside the track, which fits, since Clara Mae's father worked for the railroad; he also preached in Arcadia, according to my mother. Clara Mae had been married in Tampa in 1918, but was divorced. My mother wrote that Clara Mae worked for Granddaddy and Granny as their housekeeper.

Sometime in the 1920s, the Bells moved to Tampa, which was where Daddy was born in 1924. According to my mother, Clara Mae became a practical nurse in Tampa, and she returned to Charlotte County by 1939 for a job nursing an old man named Archie Adkins through his last illness. She would later marry his son, and then return to Tampa to work in the same Children's Home where Daddy had lived.

There was certainly reason to believe that she could be Daddy's natural mother: she had red hair and freckles, she lived next door to and worked for Granddaddy, she moved to Tampa at the time when Daddy was born there, and then she worked at the same Children's Home where Daddy had been placed.

When Clara Mae heard the rumors about herself, she wrote Granny the following letter:

> Tampa, Fla.
> Feb 1st 1939
> Mrs A.C. Frizzll:
> Dear Mrs. Frizzll:
> I certainly am surprized at all the foolish gossip going around Murdock and I will say I am not at all pleased by it. Mrs Pattie you know without a doubt that I cant have a baby. I can and will (as soon as I have the money) get my Dr to give me a statement to that effect and will gladly send it to you. I haven't ever gave birth to a child for my husband or any other man.
>
> I am truly sorry and I really never dreamed Mr F folks could be so narrow minded and in a way I am not much surprized either. They will ruin the life of an innocent child that I am sure has legal parents. I am sure you would not adopt a child that was illagimate.
>
> I have been accused unjustly many times, but some things are going just a little to far. Any one has my

permission to investige my past and find out whether or not I have ever had a child.

If you will please give me the names of the people who have done all this dirty gossip I'll thank you, for I would like very much to write them a letter, for if it does not stop and stop immadiuty I am going to take some legal steps myself. I will see if they can prove the falsehoods, and then I'll sue them for every thing they have. I could use a little money and I really think it would do some people some good to show them up for what they are worth.

I hold no hard feelings for you Mrs Frizzll. I realize how you must feel and too, just how these people can hurt the future happiness of your boy. You have my sympthy and I will do all I can to help you stop it all. I feel better knowing that you know that it isn't true.

Will you kindly show this to these low bred evil minded in laws of yours, for if they don't apoligize to me for this untruth they will certainly pay for it.
Best wishes to you and yours.

Your ever loving friend,

[signed] Clara

In 1989, a handwriting expert confirmed to my mother that the Mae Wiley, who signed the guardianship form at the Children's Home when she left Daddy there, is not the same person who wrote the above letter.

Recent DNA testing, of course, has also proven that Clara Mae Bell is NOT Daddy's real mama, but there are a lot of Frizzells who went to their graves thinking she was.

Wagging tongues are like mosquitoes. They buzz, and they buzz, and then they bite, and sometimes they leave a scar.

3615. E. Powhattan av

Tampa Fla.
Feb-1st-1939.

Mrs A. C. Frizzell:
Dear Mrs Frizzell:-
I certainly am surprized at all the foolish gossip going around Murdock. and I will say I am not at all pleased by it. Mrs Pattie you know without a doubt that I cant have a baby. I can & will (as soon as I have the money) get my Dr to give me a statement to that effect and will gladly send it to you.

In the spring of 1939, Granny resumed her position as postmistress, and Uncle Forney and his wife Annie moved to her hometown Sycamore, Georgia, where Uncle Forney would operate a grocery store and serve as mayor. Later in the year, Jack Hindman would help Granny in the store.

On September 22, Granddaddy signed his first of many Oil, Gas, and Mineral Leases. It was with Peninsula Oil and Refining Corporation for a period of ten years on 1,250 acres of land that Granddaddy owned south of Punta Gorda. The annual rental was $62.50 with royalties paid to him in the amount of 1/8 for oil and gas and 1/10 for minerals.

September 24, 1939
Eighteen extra good farm mules
at Frizzell Lumber Co., Immokalee, Fla.

In October, Granddaddy bought most of the land between the El Jobean tract and Murdock and most of the land surrounding Mars to the east of Murdock. It totaled around 10,000 acres.

Earlier in the year, he had also bought 200 acres northwest of his El Jobean tract. He bought it from Joel Bean with the understanding that if Joel repaid the price within ninety days at eight percent interest, then he would get the land back.

In November, large delegations of cattlemen, public officials, and others from all sections of the state attended a Florida pasture and cattle tour through ten central and southern Florida counties. The purpose of the tour was to show the citizens of Florida and other states the progress and stability of the Florida range cattle industry. The last stop on the tour was Granddaddy's ranch at noon for a barbecue of the beef that had been fattened on his new experimental pasture grasses.

By then, Granddaddy had a herd of buffalo on his ranch, too. Daniel happened to see a fine, smoky red one about two years old and thought it was the finest looking animal of the "cow tribe" at Murdock that he had ever seen.

That Christmas, Granddaddy and Granny hosted another barbecue dinner, this one for friends and family. They served roast beef, roast pork, swamp cabbage, pig knuckles, pickles, bread, fruit salad, coffee.

"MILLION-DOLLAR SUCCESS STORY"

... the story of a working couple who built a 200,000-acre ranch.

January 10, 1940
NOTES payable to R. B. Mayer bearing my signature have been stolen. All parties are requested not to honor this paper. Please wire collect if presented.
A. C. Frizzell, Immokalee, Fla.

The year 1940 began with Granddaddy now living in Immokalee near his sawmill and visiting Granny on the weekends in Murdock, while Daddy was preparing to leave for military school in February.

In an effort to fill the upcoming loneliness in her life, Granny wrote a letter to The Children's Home in Tampa. In it, she requested a female companion/helper, perhaps a surrogate daughter.

Murdock, Fla. 1/23/40
Children Home -
Tampa, Fla. -
... we adopted one of your boys Paul Wylie, now our boy is fifteen years old, a fine, manly boy and we are sending him to Kentucky Military Institute on Feb 6th, to give him the best advantage we can to have a good education. He has been my standby for past six years as his Daddy has been at Mill greater part of time leaving us at home.

I really need some one in house with me at night. My housekeeper and colored woman lives in yard close to house. I wondered if you had a girl say ten or 12 maybe 8 to 10 that would be a help to me and let me be a help to her. My age [69th birthday 3 days before] forbids my offering to adopt a child but for a while at least maybe permanently I could give her a good home and send her to school. Then another thought even a high school steady, of well established habits could stay with me and finish Hi. I would in no wise treat a girl as a servant - just want her to do the things a daughter rightly raised would want to do for Mother.

I have a modern home fully equiped with electricity telephone, bus to Punta Gorda goes in front of house - Sunday school and church near. All week there would be no one at home but she and I. Mr F comes in Sat. night and goes back to Mill Monday.

I notice so many women Mothers want help in Tpa [Tampa], the idea occurred to me, if the above idea could not be worked out I might find a white woman, who would be willing to come here and do my little work for a home for herself and one child and $15.00 per month, or if not willing to do laundry (I have a washing machine, electric iron) can pay $10.00 and board her and child under ten years.

Please see what you can do for me.

This does not mean I would dispense with my cook I have if I got a girl. Would have to keep a cook and laundress.

Yours truly,
[signed] Mrs. A. C. Frizzell

The Superintendent replied that she was glad to hear Daddy was having "such a splendid educational opportunity" and had "been such a real pleasure and help to" Granny. She said that she would get together her Board members and try to find a girl for Granny. If there was no one at the home, she would contact the Child Welfare Center, where someone might be able to find a "nice mother and a child, who might fit." She then thanked Granny for what she had done for Daddy and for her request for a little girl to help.

Starting February 2, 1940, for the second half of Daddy's ninth grade and all of his tenth and eleventh grades, he attended Kentucky Military Institute, one of the oldest military preparatory schools in the United States. Its main campus was near Louisville, Kentucky, and its winter campus was in Venice, Florida, about 25 miles northwest of Murdock.

K. M. I. had uniforms for both Kentucky and Florida, the main difference being white pants for Florida. On the left in front of the Murdock store, Daddy is wearing his Kentucky fatigues, or combat dress uniform. On the right, he is wearing his Kentucky "Old West Point Style" full-dress uniform. Notice his hat.

While Daddy was away at school that year, Granddaddy expanded his operations at the Arzell sawmill and at the Murdock ranch. In the spring, he signed a lease with Atlantic Coastline Railroad for about five miles of sidetrack from the railroad to his sawmill, and in the fall, he leased a sizable parcel of pastureland west of the Myakka River from Justine Sweat for the grazing of cattle. The lease included the use of a house, barn, and sheds. With his expansions came more employees, and they totaled over 150 by then.

At Christmastime that year, Daniel saw Granny and Daddy at the Mercantile. Granny proudly displayed the Frizzell success. "She was wearing nice jewelry, wrist watch, diamonds. Paul was home for the holidays. He greeted me."

Throughout the year while Granddaddy was expanding his sawmill operation and his ranch, he had continued expanding his land holdings. He bought about 10,000 more acres of land north of Murdock, most of it along the northern Charlotte County line, and some of it extending into Sarasota County with 1,000 acres in the North Port area, all highlighted in red on the map that follows.

In the next year 1941, in addition to about a dozen parcels scattered throughout the county, he made one sizable purchase in September for 2,130 more acres in the Charlotte Harbor area. The land was pretty much all that was left for him to buy between the two rivers on the southwest side of Highway 41. It is highlighted in blue on the map. He bought it for $4 per acre for a total of $8,520, payable $1,130 down and three annual payments at six percent interest.

With the exception of a few small parcels owned by others, the below map shows roughly 30,000 acres, or 50 square miles, of land between the two rivers that Granddaddy owned by the end of 1941. Land outside of Charlotte County, as well as other Charlotte County land owned by him in and near Punta Gorda, McCall, and Englewood is not shown.

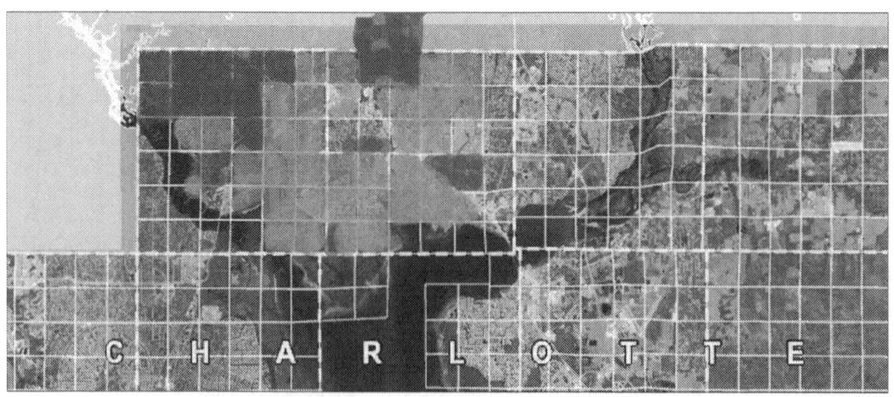

Frizzell Property 1941 in Blue, 1940 in Red, Previous Years in Green
(Charlotte County Section Map Transformed).

The year 1941 ended with the United States entering World War II. On December 7, the Japanese bombed Pearl Harbor, and the next day, the United States and Britain declared war on Japan. Then on December 11, Hitler declared war on the United States.

Although war had been raging in Europe for over two years, the United States had been involved only to the extent that it had contributed military aid to its allies. Now, it would contribute men. Now, it would actively and aggressively enter into a war that stretched across the globe. It would call over ten million American men to battle, and almost a half a million would not return home.

With the United States rapidly mobilizing both its human and material resources, on May 18, 1942, at the end of Daddy's eleventh grade, the Director of Admissions for Kentucky Military Institute wrote Granny:

> Dear Mrs. Frizzell:
>
> In view of the practical certainty that all young men will be called to active military service sooner or later, we assume that you will wish to have Paul return to K. M. I. to continue his officer's training course along with his general education, the better to prepare for that military service when it comes.
>
> Paul has done creditable work in his studies this year, he has conformed cheerfully to the regulations and has conducted himself as a gentleman. He has taken part in school activities and doubtless is developing along the right lines. We believe that Paul has in him the makings of a mighty fine man. Consequently, we invite him to return next year, and we hope very much that you and Mr. Frizzell plan to send him.
>
> ...

The rest of the letter asked if he would be returning and announced a tuition increase.

In light of the probability that he would be called to war before the end of his senior year, Daddy did not return to K. M. I.; in the fall, he attended Charlotte High School in Punta Gorda. There, he played as a guard on the Fighting Tarpons varsity football team, and he broke his nose during one of the games.

In that year of 1942, since Granddaddy had already bought most of the land on the west side of Highway 41, he had started buying land on the east side. He bought 4,640 acres in Sarasota County north of where Veterans Boulevard is today; he bought 360 acres in what is now Port Charlotte between Kensington Street and Harbor Boulevard; and he bought over 2,000 acres at what is now the intersection of I75 and Kings Highway.

Then in October, he and Granny deeded to Daddy forty acres of the Kings Highway property for him to start his own ranch. Daddy had already accumulated over 800 cattle and horses in his own right.

The following month on November 2, Granddaddy's long-time friend, Joel Bean, died at his El Jobean home in the town he had founded. After a long illness, he died a pauper at the age of 75.

Granddaddy paid for his funeral and arranged to have him buried with other local pioneers at the Indian Springs Cemetery south of Punta Gorda on Alligator Creek.

A couple of months after the death of his close friend, Granddaddy appeared in a Miami courtroom, where a federal judge ruled against him. On January 21, 1943, the judge permanently enjoined the A. C. Frizzell Lumber Company from violating the wage and hour act. The company agreed to pay 168 employees back wages that totaled $2,815 in varying amounts from 20 cents to $213 each.[1]

Perhaps Arzell Sawmill had run its course by then, but Granddaddy did immediately close it after the judge's ruling and after ten years of operation. He would still be busy in the Immokalee area, though, with a watermelon farm that he had started there.

> January 24, 1943
> FOR SALE - One power drive 80 horse International power unit, been used 60 days. One 25 Woods 6x15 Matcher. One American 4 block carriage Saw Mill, Tower Edger, complete with pulleys, shafting, belting. Frizzell Lumber Co., Immokalee, Fla.

A couple of weeks later, Daddy conferred Power of Attorney to Granddaddy, and on February 16, at the age of 18 with only a few months left before he would have graduated from Charlotte High, he entered the armed services at Camp Blanding, Florida. After two weeks there, he transferred to boot camp at Ft. McClellan, near Anniston, Alabama, where he trained for almost three months. He then took a train to Camp Shenango in western Pennsylvania, a holding point for trained soldiers awaiting deployment. Three weeks later, he traveled to Camp Patrick Henry, Virginia, where he stayed for two weeks, not knowing where he would go next. There, he endured hardcore mental training and learned to "Kill or be Killed."

After five months of training in the U. S., on July 14, 1943, Daddy boarded a train for Newport News, Virginia, where he walked the plank of a large troop ship that transported him to Casablanca, Africa, a week later. In North Africa, he spent two months of intensive training to prepare for fighting in Italy, "where only good troops with good training would survive.[2]"

In Italy, he would spend two years fighting on the front lines as a heavy machine gunner in the 133rd Regiment of the 34th Red Bull Infantry Division of the 5th Army. He would fight his way northward through Italy's peninsula for 450 miles, and then for 400 miles across northern Italy, much of it walking and carrying his own equipment.

An account of his World War II experience is detailed in my book entitled *In the Face of Obstacles*.

About the time that Daddy landed in Casablanca, Annabel's daughter, Martha Pearle, who was Daddy's age, married George Vogt, who was age 24 at the time. They would stay married for sixty-eight years, until they both died in 2011. They lived in Orlando, and they had three children. In 1963, they started the very successful Vogt Realty.

Martha Pearle would become "accomplished in the art of needlework and was certified by the Elsa Williams School of Needle Art. She traveled to Japan in pursuit of [a] Graduation Certificate by learning the 46 basic [techniques in a course for] Traditional Japanese Embroidery. She traveled to Perthshire, Scotland, to research and co-author the needlework of Lady Evelyn Murray."[1]

Three Generations
Granny, Annabel, Martha Pearle, "ca 1940."

A couple of months later, after two months of training in North Africa, Daddy had only been in Italy for ten days when he was shot in the leg on October 2 in a battle at Benevento. From there, he was carried by mule for sixty miles through the snowy mountains to Naples on the coast, where he was loaded onto a ship and transported 400 miles across the Mediterranean to a hospital in North Africa. He stayed there for two months, before returning to Naples to rejoin his regiment. From Naples, he then spent a month fighting in the snow-covered mountains on his way to Cassino, where he fought in the bloodiest and deadliest battle of them all.

Daddy at Naples, Italy, in December 1943.
"To Mom and Dad from your loving son."

That fall, while Daddy was in the North Africa hospital, Granddaddy was establishing Punta Gorda Motor Sales, "selling and servicing Ford cars, trucks and tractors, and carrying a complete line of parts to service them. Also selling farm implements."[4] He called it the Ford Place, and it was located on Marion Avenue in the old H. W. Smith Building, now on the National Register of Historical Places.

Then in December, after the Ford Place was up and running, he partnered with Guy Johnson and bought Hunter's Drug Store on First Street in Ft. Myers. Established in 1905, it was the oldest drug store in Ft. Myers and the second oldest store. Granddaddy was a silent partner in the business, while Guy managed it. Granddaddy, no doubt, had met Guy in Immokalee, where Guy was in the mercantile business for a few years, after having managed a store in Tallahassee.

Building on Marion Avenue, where Granddaddy's Ford Place once was, 2015.

Interior view of the Hunter Drug store - Fort Myers, Florida. 19--.
Black & white photoprint, 8 x 10 in. State Archives of Florida, Florida Memory.
<https://www.floridamemory.com/items/show/38022>, (accessed 28 April 2018).

The year 1944 began with Granny's health continuing to fail, and by March she left Murdock and went to Ft. Myers, where she spent two weeks at the Bradford Hotel. She left the hotel on March 28 and entered Lee Memorial Hospital, where she stayed for a month.

> May 13, 1944
> Wanted at once, man and wife for yardman and housekeeper cook for family of two. One must drive car. Five-room house, all modern conveniences, located on Tamiami Trail 8 miles from Punta Gorda. Telephone and telegraph connections. Wife semi-invalid, husband away from home greater part of time. Room, board, and good wages for right parties. No laundry. Reference. Write or call phone 103L, Punta Gorda, A. C. Frizzell, Murdock, Fla.

The month of May was a landmark month for Granddaddy. It was then that he became one of Florida's largest landowners, when he bought from the Ringling Brothers a total of about 35,000 acres in Sarasota County. His ranch would now extend well into Sarasota County.

Following the purchase, he signed oil, gas, and mineral leases for 35 cents per acre for rights on about 68,000 acres in Sarasota and Charlotte Counties. Each lease was for so much down, so much per year, and royalties on any product.

Earlier in the year, he had bought 1,000 acres along Highway 41 near Charlotte Harbor, and he signed another oil, gas, and mineral lease for the rights for ten years on 15,000+ acres of his land in what would later be Port Charlotte.

May would also be a landmark month for Daddy, when on the 29th, he was wounded for a second time, this time at Anzio near Rome. A medical flight transported him to a Naples hospital, and he was still there on July 15, when he received the Combat Infantryman Badge. The badge had been created during World War II as "primary recognition of the combat service and sacrifices of infantrymen who would likely be wounded or killed in numbers disproportionate to those of soldiers from the Army's other service branches." He is wearing it under his purple heart lapel pin in the below photo. That fall, after he recuperated, he rejoined his regiment, and he spent the winter fighting in the snowy Apennine Mountains of Italy under extremely harsh conditions.

"To the best Mom and Dad a boy ever had. Your son, Paul."

Perhaps the news of Daddy's second wound sent Granddaddy into a buying frenzy for the remainder of that year. He bought 640 more acres on Kings Highway, 80+ acres west of the Myakka River, and another parcel in Charlotte Harbor on Highway 41. He bought the Royal Palm Music Service in Ft. Myers. He bought over 1,000 acres along the northern Charlotte County line, 80 acres at 65 cents per acre on the Bermont Road about five miles east of Punta Gorda, and various lots in El Jobean, Punta Gorda, and Murdock, including two in Murdock for $5.00 each. He bought Joel Bean's house on the Myakka River in El Jobean for $3,275. Joel Bean had bought the house in the 1930s, after living in his hotel when the depression hit.

Granddaddy also bought almost all that was left of the platted Murdock lots at the intersection of Highways 776 and 41. On the below map, the blue lots were purchased in the summer, the green were purchased at the end of the year, and the pink were previous purchases.

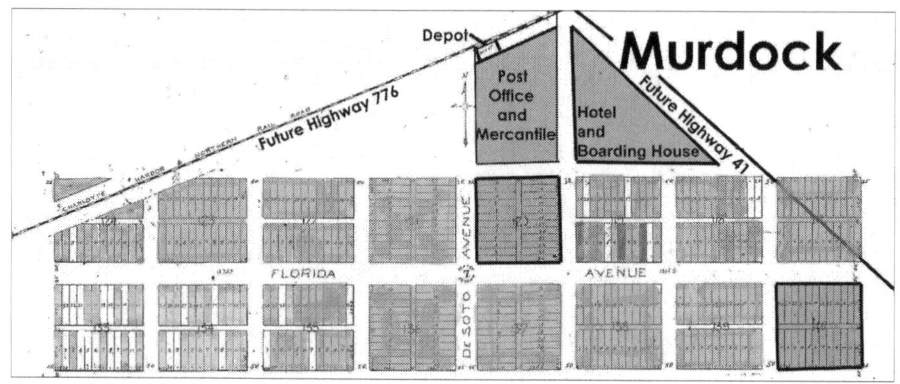

Platted Murdock lots owned by Granddaddy as of the end of 1944
(1914 Murdock Plat Map Transformed).

In the middle of his buying frenzy, he demolished the boarding house, over forty years old, that had served as the Frizzell family home for so long.

> October 23, 1944, Sarasota Herald Tribune
> SIXTEEN ROOM wooden building to be wrecked and moved. Good lumber.
> A. C. Frizzell, Murdock, Fla.

Granddaddy's buying frenzy continued into 1945 when in April, he purchased a 12,000-acre ranch from a Texan. It was located in Beverly Acres, seven miles east of the Peace River on the Desoto and Charlotte County line, about where "The Farm" Recreation Center is now on Highway 31. The property was formerly known as Charlotte Hereford Ranch, and he bought all of the cattle (about 900 head), two horses and three saddles, plus all machinery and equipment owned by the seller and used in the operation of the ranch.

It was in that same month, when a neighbor told Daniel that Granddaddy was now in the "millionaire class." They had been talking about a Bill to Quiet Title between Granddaddy and John M. Murdock and others. It had appeared in the Herald beginning on March 1 for all of those Murdock lots that Granddaddy had bought the year before.

Granddaddy had become a millionaire at a time when millionaires were rare. There were only 13,000 millionaires in the entire United States in 1945; today, there are eleven million.

At the same time that Granddaddy was buying the Charlotte Hereford Ranch and 900 more beef cattle, Granny sent two egg recipes to *The Tampa Tribune* with the idea of using eggs as a meat replacement for meals other than breakfast. Meat had been rationed for two years since shortly after the U. S. entered the war, but poultry and eggs had not been. Meat had been rationed, because it was being sent to soldiers overseas and to newly liberated countries that were too war-torn to produce their own. Now, it was so scarce that it would not be sent to the liberated countries for three months, and Americans were encouraged to observe "Meatless Tuesdays."

Granny received praise from two *Tribune* judges who called her recipes "interesting and easy new ways to put eggs onto the table." Granny, "timely person that she is," had sent her ideas that were "two family favorites," but certainly not substitutes by Granddaddy or Daddy for a two-inch thick, juicy, grilled T-bone steak.

> 1. Cut green onion tops fine, add a small amount of water and a tablespoon of shortening to each quart of tops. Let simmer until fat becomes quite hot, add three or four well beaten eggs and scramble together until eggs are creamy. Serve at once. (Don't start off with too much water. A steaming amount does the trick.)
>
> 2. For a quick vegetable dish, scramble three eggs with the vegetables from canned vegetable soup, and a tablespoon of shortening. Makes a colorful and appetizing dish.[5]

About four months later, the war finally ended, and on August 22, 1945, Daddy arrived in Boston by ship. His ship had left Italy and was off the coast of Gibraltar headed for the Pacific war zone, when it received the news and changed course for the U. S. A.

Two months later, Daddy was discharged at Camp Blanding, Florida, as a Private First Class. He had served in the military for two years and eight months with no furloughs. His total pay was $300, and he received a payment of $100 plus $17.20 travel pay upon discharge.

He had survived a campaign in Italy that had killed 114,000 American men and over 300,000 Italian men. He had walked into the war, a teenage high school boy, and walked out, a 21-year-old man who had experienced firsthand man's inhumanity to man. His gentle spirit had not changed, but he had learned that life beyond the barbed wire fence of his daddy's ranch was tainted with unimaginable horror and evil. He was happy to return to the confines of the ranch, where the only slaughtering was that of cattle.

During Daddy's absence, Granddaddy had continued business as usual, at times with a fury, but for the most part, seemingly unaffected by the war. His prestige had grown significantly, though, and his influence had spread throughout southern Florida from Orlando to Tampa to Miami. He was well-known and respected by all who knew him, including Florida's most prominent citizens.

On October 5, his community standing was affirmed when he was elected to the Board of Directors of the Punta Gorda State Bank, which had joined a state chain. He would be re-elected in January of every year until his death.

Three weeks later, it was business as usual when he shipped ten cars of cattle to Swift and Company in Orlando.

> November 1, 1945
> WHITE housekeeper cook for family of 3 adults. Living on ranch located on railroad and highway. No laundry. Pay $18 per wk. Private room and board.
> A. C. Frizzell, Murdock, Fla.

The year 1945 had begun in January with Daddy on the battlefield and now ended in December with him on the football field. He played tackle in the starting lineup for the ninth Fish Bowl game in Punta Gorda between alumni all-star football teams from the Punta Gorda and Arcadia high schools.[6]

After returning from the war, Daddy seemed to find peace and tranquility on the ranch. One day, Daniel rode with him "and a colored man in the Lincoln-Zephyr 4-door. Paul says he is living at home, but is most of the time in the woods with the cowboys except at night."

By the beginning of 1946, the ranch was bustling with activity. Daniel wrote that the cowboys were handling cattle at the pens, and others on horseback were driving a bunch along the highway in heavy traffic.

Frizzell Cow Pens.

In March, Daniel helped Fred Quednau pick up about a dozen pairs of horns at the Frizzell butcher lot, and Fred gave him a beef tail. Fred had been talking to Granddaddy at the pens. While they were talking, Daniel had counted six fresh hides that Inspector J. S. Goff was checking. Men were marking meat and loading it onto a truck. Mrs. Goff and another woman were there, both in pants. Quite a herd of cattle were being taken north from the pens, and a big trailer also had a load to take.

> April 10, 1946
> WANTED - White Southern woman to cook and keep house clean for three adults, five-room house in country. Room, board and good wages to right party. Must be honest, sober and industrious.
> Mrs. A. C. Frizzell, Murdock, Florida.

Surely Granny received an overwhelming response to her above classified ad that offered room and board at a time when the country was undergoing a severe housing shortage. Within a few months of the war's end, housing demand had risen dramatically when wartime industries converted to peacetime productions, personal incomes were being maintained, and the marriage rate was rising. Veterans were returning to the cities, not to the farms of the depression era prior to the war; they did not need to grow their own food in order to survive now. They were thriving, and they were marrying and starting families. Housing was in high demand.

Granny wrote *The Tampa Tribune* that the present housing shortage reminded her of the railroad car homes that she had devised for herself and her two children when she worked in New Mexico years ago at the turn of the century, before she met Granddaddy.

> While we were waiting for the El Paso and Southwestern Railroad to complete the depot and agent's quarters, the children and I were very comfortable in a caboose that was not in road condition.
>
> We had a nice kitchenette with sufficient shelving for groceries and utensils. Two beds were in one end of the cab, and the cupola was our sitting room. With pretty dimity curtains and the seats covered with cretonne, we lived in comfort and I was able to have my children with me.
>
> True, we were 60 miles from the nearest town, but with 12 to 20 trains passing daily, we had no time to get lonely.
>
> After being transferred by the railroad to a small limestone mining center, "we had to live a mile from the depot, but this didn't suit me, as I wanted the children with me. So the railroad gave us two abandoned box cars. I put them together with an

eight-foot hall, put a high roof over them, and cut the partition out of the front and rear of each car to make two rooms, one 16 by 16 feet and the other 28 by 16 feet.

We also had a nice front and side porch, and a fireplace in the rear of the hall. We lived comfortably and happily in the box cars for four years, at which time we were transferred.

> It isn't the houses where you come from nor the places you stay that makes for happiness, but the ability to make a home when and where you can make a living.[7]

While Granny was reminiscing about her railroad car homes, Granddaddy was out drinking and got into trouble on the highway. On April 13, he forfeited a bond for $10 for reckless driving. His case was one of twenty-one that went before the vice-mayor in a Ft. Myers police court.[8]

May 7, 1946, Ft. Myers News-Press
STRAYED OR STOLEN - from A. C. Frizzell's Ranch late Sunday P. M. A female Leopard dog. 14 mos. old. Has gray and black spots with reddish cast. Name is Michelle. Wore collar with A. F. stamped on it. Reward for information leading to recovery or delivery to Frizzell's Ranch, Murdock, Fla.

In July, Daddy was hurt by a bull, and on the 18th, he was discharged from Lee Memorial Hospital. Daniel wrote, "Out now, but not well. Injury in several ribs."

December 14, 1946
FOR SALE - Brahma bulls; 20 head coming, 2 years old, registered Brahma bulls, shipped from Hungerford, Texas, 30 days ago.
A. C. Frizzell, Murdock, Fla.

A few days after Granddaddy placed the above ad, Granny was admitted to Lee Memorial Hospital, where she stayed for four days. She returned home to Murdock in time to give Daniel a "large box of home-made candy" on Christmas Day.

At some point in the past year since Daddy had returned from the war, he received an honorary diploma from Charlotte High School in Punta Gorda. Many World War II veterans who had been recruited from high school received such diplomas. Daddy's diploma was dated June 4, 1943, the date when he would have graduated. On that day, he was in Ft. McClellan, Alabama, training for the war.

After he received his diploma, at the strong suggestion of Granddaddy, he began the year 1947 by continuing his education at Tampa Business College. "The school's mission was to provide practical education in areas of business such as bookkeeping and standard shorthand. The school was open all year long and was the most up to date in the South. College departments included Business/Bookkeeping, Stenography/Typewriting, Telegraphy, Penmanship, and English.[9]"

Daddy attended classes during the week, and on the weekends, he rode a bus a hundred miles home to Murdock. On one of those weekends, he went to a dance in Punta Gorda at a community hall in a rustic, cypress-log building in the Municipal Trailer Park. It was located on the bay across the Tamiami Trail from the Hotel Charlotte Harbor. At the dance, he met my mother, Sandra Elizabeth Claire, and a whirlwind romance ensued. Only a few Friday nights later, on Valentine's Day, he gave her a ring with a solitary diamond.

Daddy, at age 22, had been working on the ranch for about a year since he returned from almost two years of World War II horror in Italy; Mother, at age 19, had just completed two and a half years of college in Michigan. With an IQ of 165, she had skipped two grades in her earlier education. Her parents were both college graduates and highly intelligent. Her father was a retired electrical engineer, and her mother had started teaching at the Charlotte Harbor Schoolhouse soon after their arrival in Punta Gorda that winter.

The two of them had traveled from Michigan to Punta Gorda with their three children and with mother's grandma. My mother's younger brother was only six, and her sister was three. The six of them were living in a trailer that measured about eighteen feet in length.

Mother wrote about her first arrival in Florida.

> My parents (Vivian Ranta Gorton and Olen Joseph "O. J." Claire) moved to Florida when I went off to college. They returned to Michigan the next summer, and then waited until my fall term ended, about December 15, 1946. At that point, we headed south with Grandma Gorton, my small brother, Earl, and sister, Carol.
>
> We went to Biloxi, Mississippi, first, after ten days of traveling in a snowstorm all the way, pulling a mobile home behind the car. We arrived in Biloxi on Christmas Eve. We spent a few weeks there, and I joined the U. S. O.
>
> Then we came to Florida for the balance of the winter.

They parked their little trailer in Punta Gorda at the trailer park near the community hall where Daddy and Mother met. The trailer park had opened in the 1930's and attracted guests for the same reasons as the hotel that shadowed it: the climate and the fishing.

Locals called the park's winter residents "tin can tourists," who "brought a shirt and a five-dollar bill and did not change either all winter."[10] Over the years, many locals would prosper from their "tin can tourists," but they did so with resentment and without considering the consequences.

Ten days after their Valentine engagement, on Monday, February 24, 1947, Daddy and Mother eloped to Bainbridge, Georgia, where a judge married them. They announced their marriage in the Punta Gorda paper, and Granddaddy and Granny hosted a reception for them at their Murdock home on March 8.

Between 140 and 150 guests attended the old southern barbecue supper that was served on the lawn. Among the guests were two captains from Kentucky Military Institute. Vocal selections, with piano accompaniment, included "I Love You Truly" and "Always." "Always" was the newlywed couple's song.

After the reception, Mother returned to school with Daddy in Tampa. They lived in a house at 416 Hugh Street. News of their marriage did not escape the school newspaper.

> One of the veterans thought there was a romance going on between two of our new students who sit in the front part of the large study hall. Mr. and Mrs. A.F. seem to spend an enjoyable day studying bookkeeping together. "Must be Newlyweds!"

Within a month, they left Tampa to live in Murdock, where they moved into a white frame house across the railroad track from the Mercantile on the same side of Highway 41.

Granddaddy had sent Daddy to school to learn bookkeeping, that being the first step in preparing him to one day take over his empire, but Daddy had no interest in bookkeeping. He did not want to study it, and so he dropped out.

He went back to work for Granddaddy doing various jobs on the ranch. He worked with the cattle. He worked as Murdock postmaster for about four months, and he worked in the store. He helped Uncle Johnnie with the pasture improvement program that Granddaddy had started in 1937, but had temporarily halted during the war.

Mother went to work for Granddaddy, too. "My husband was paid $50 a month during the 1940's for working with the cattle, and I was paid seven dollars for helping with the books and doing secretarial work. We usually owed most of our $57 a month to the company store, so once you started working for old A. C., it was sort of difficult to break away."

On April 7, Granddaddy and Granny gave Daddy and Mother a quarter horse from Texas for a wedding gift. The roan-colored stallion had his own private corral in the backyard. Daddy named him Sandy, which is what he called Mother, a nickname derived from her first name, Sandra.

"Paul Frizzell, Cattleman and Cowboy, on his prized horse - 'Sandy', near his cattle truck."

Sandy.

That same month, Granddaddy collided his car with some of his own cattle on the highway between Murdock and Charlotte Harbor. He went to the Ft. Myers hospital in shock with a badly bruised jaw and stayed there for three days. His car was demolished.

Three months later in July, he had another car accident and returned to the hospital with both shoulders dislocated; at the end of the month, Granny followed him to the hospital to spend three weeks there for her heart condition.

> April 27, 1947
> WOOD FOR SALE - Can furnish 500 to 1000 cords good lightwood for orange groves at $9 per cord FOB cars. A. C. Frizzell, Murdock, Fla.

Florida growers sometimes used fat lightwood to protect orange groves during a freeze. It outlasted petroleum pots to keep the trees warm. The growers would build a wall of fire on one side of the grove, and it would burn for three days with great warmth, occasionally burning the first row of trees, turning them into pyramids of fire, but saving the rest of the grove from the freeze.

That summer of 1947 was uneventful, until September 17, when the Ft. Lauderdale Hurricane, also known as the Pompano Beach Hurricane, swept through South Florida with peak gusts of 155 miles per hour. It would hold the record for the highest measured wind speed in Florida before Hurricane Andrew.

The hurricane slowly moved across the state at a speed of about ten miles per hour, and it dropped rainfall that set single-month records, some of which still stand today. The flooding was among the worst in South Florida's history, and water remained standing in many places for months.[11]

Although a new dike had held around Lake Okeechobee, but would need reinforcement afterward, the Everglades had flooded and the surviving cattle in that area were starving. The government paid other Florida ranchers to room and board the cattle. Daddy rode on Sandy, assisted by the ranch cowboys, and they rescued 1,000 head to graze on the ranch, until the floodwaters subsided. They drove the cattle westward and then down Highway 41 south of Venice.

Daddy on Sandy with 1,000 cows on both sides of Highway 41, near Venice, October 26, 1947.

December 7, 1947
4 Ft. Clean Lightwood FOR SALE $9 PER CORD
F. O. B. Saline, Florida
A. C. FRIZZELL, Murdock, Florida

In the beginning of December, Mother was still working for Granddaddy in his Mercantile office, but by the middle of the month, she spent most of her time in bed for the last six weeks of her first pregnancy, which was with me. She was tall and slim, and her health was frail, although there was nothing frail about her personality.

At the same time, Granny's heart condition was worsening, and by January, she was confined to bed, too, where she passed the time reading newspapers, books, and Western Romance magazines. Granny was another case of frail health and strong personality. She would be in the hospital at the same time that Mother was there giving birth to me, but Granny would stay for about three months. Her condition was so bad that Granddaddy's brother, Forney, and sister, Lizzie, traveled from out of state to be there.

Two bedridden women, however, did not deter Granddaddy from attending a two-day Ocala Brahman Cattle Show on January 9. It started with a colorful parade through downtown Ocala in the morning and ended with record prices for twenty-six Brahmans at the fourth annual sale of the Southeastern Brahman Breeders Association. The large livestock pavilion was packed with a crowd that cheered when the auctioneers announced the new records. The average price for a bull was $888.65, but Granddaddy paid $1,000 for one from a Bartow ranch.[12]

On February 3, I was born in Lee Memorial Hospital in Ft. Myers. The Charlotte Hospital in Punta Gorda would have been more convenient, but it had just opened in August, and it only had twelve beds, along with an emergency room, x-ray room, and laboratory.

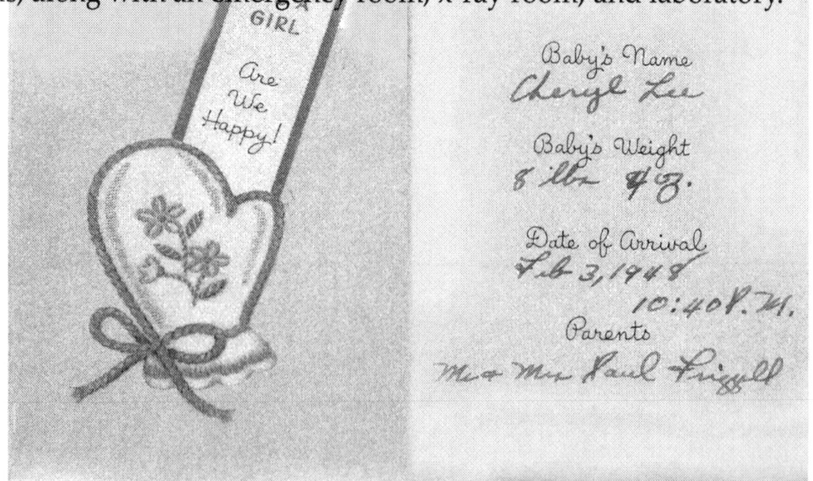

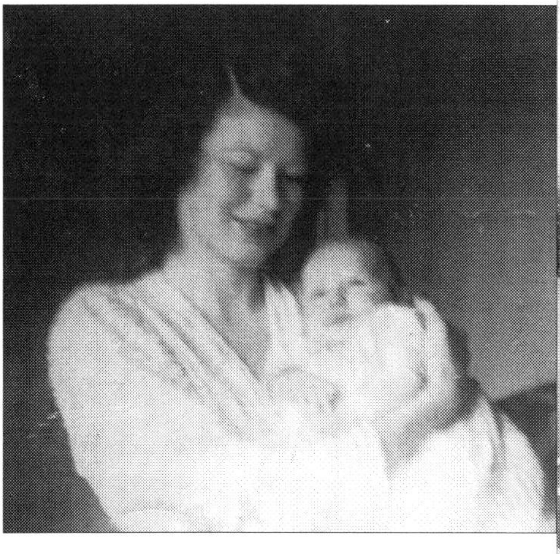

Mable

Three months later, Granny was discharged from the hospital.

May 26, 1948, Ft. Myers News Press

CARD OF THANKS

I wish to express my sincere thanks and appreciation to my dear friends and relatives for their many kindnesses during my illness. I wish to especially thank the Lee Memorial Hospital Staff, Doctors and Nurses, for going far beyond the line of duty in caring for me. Also last but certainly not least, I wish to thank the Ft. Myers Coca Cola Company for having my paper delivered to me daily.

Mrs. Pattie B. Frizzell

Murdock, Florida

In June, Granddaddy and Uncle Johnnie both registered for a 1948 government allotment restricted to $500 each for participation in the 1947 Federal Soil Conservation Program. While most payments in Charlotte County were for vegetable and citrus land, theirs was for extensive pasture improvement work.[13]

Then in July, Granddaddy gave Uncle Johnnie's older son, 10-year-old Preston, a young 425-pound bay stallion and a new junior size stock saddle that was "just Preston's fit," according to Daniel.

Around the first of August, Daddy and Mother headed for Michigan to introduce me to my northern relatives, most of whom Daddy had not met yet, either. On our return trip to Florida, we stopped at the Natural Bridge of Virginia before traveling down the Blue Ridge Parkway through the Appalachian Mountains of North Carolina. It was the first of many family summer trips North.

While we were gone, on August 13, Granddaddy shipped rodeo calves to Texas, after Mexican calves had been quarantined there for cattle fever tick infestation. He was the second rancher in Sarasota and Charlotte counties to ship calves to Texas cattle dealers for use in rodeos. His shipment of 114 cross-bred Brahman calves was the larger of the two, the first being only thirty-five. He shipped them by truck to San Angelo, Texas, where they were to be used for roping in rodeo shows. He sold them for $5,000 or 22 cents per pound. He planned to ship about 1,000 by October 1st.[14]

"Cherry on Preston's horse."

A couple of weeks later, on August 29, an article about Granddaddy and Granny filled an entire page of *The Tampa Sunday Tribune,* the "Million-Dollar Success Story" of a working couple who built a 200,000-acre ranch. By then, they ranked near the top of Florida's list of big ranchers. They had thousands of head of cattle grazing on 200,000 acres, all fenced, in Sarasota and Charlotte counties. They owned over 100,000 acres, and they had grazing leases for another 100,000 acres. Land and cattle holdings were worth over a million dollars at that time (ten million today).

Granny was in ill health and did not get around the ranch holdings, as she had in the years past. She was "effervescent," "in fine spirits, a gay conversationalist, and enjoyed 'talking the cow business.'"

Granddaddy was still working in timber, but cattle formed the largest part of his assets. "Today, I guess, most of my herd is three-quarters Brahman, and I like the Brahman blood. I can't get too much of the Brahman blood in my cattle to suit me, but I want some of the Angus around, too.

"I have had some top calves, weighing 300 to 350 pounds at weaning time, out of my Brahman cows by the Angus bulls, and they all came like the Angus, too, black and butt-headed."

Although he shipped many cattle to "feeders" in the West, Granddaddy preferred marketing them at the Arcadia auction. "Yes, sir, I'm for the auctions. I can make more money hauling animals to Arcadia than I can selling them to the packer buyers on the ranch."

With his herd of "outstanding purebred registered Brahmans," Granddaddy provided many Florida ranches with quality stock for upgrading herds.

At the time of the article, Daddy rode the range at the head of a crew of ten men, but Granddaddy did not ride horses. He said that he was too busy to do much riding. He checked his cowhands by automobile and did not miss a thing.

A few days before, the Hercules Powder Company had started clearing stumps from Granddaddy's land and shipping them to its processing plants in Jacksonville.

Granddaddy said, "Heck, I guess they'll be working around here on my stuff for four or five years."

Granddaddy had contracted with Hercules to remove the fat pine stumps from 100,000 acres. The company was clearing about 500 acres per week and expected to double it when the rainy season ended. After the stumps were removed, Granddaddy planned to put the land in shape for improved pasture grasses by chopping and plowing the native vegetation with two new tractors and choppers. [15]

That fall, Granddaddy continued an ongoing effort to prepare Daddy for taking over the Frizzell empire some day. He put him to work at his Ford Place in Punta Gorda, but Daddy did not stay there long. He was out of his element there, just as he was when he was working in the Mercantile.

Experience in the bookkeeping business world, especially in the Mercantile, had launched Granddaddy's illustrious career, and he expected the same for Daddy. And so, Daddy had studied bookkeeping for those few months at Tampa Business College, but he did not have an interest in it, and he did not have the strong personality of, or the inclination to be, a business manager. He had worked in the Mercantile off and on for a year now, and he had worked at the Ford Place, but there was only one place where he was happy, and that was working with the cattle on the ranch.

He was a cowboy. His true place in life was on the ranch, riding horses on the range and working with the cattle. He was at one with the wild country of Southwest Florida. That was his element. When my Uncle Earl remembers Daddy on the ranch, he calls him *The Marlboro Man*. He was.

Daddy "with purebred Brahmas in the cow pens at Murdock" 1948.

Mother, on the other hand, was a city girl, who excelled at bookkeeping, and she prepared an accounting of the ranch for 1948. Ranch annual income totaled $237,000.00 (over $2,000,000 today), which included income from cattle, gladiola land, hunting rights, oil lease, and tar. Taxes totaled $15,056.48, which included Charlotte and Sarasota County land and personal property. Expenses included ten men who were "kept as permanent help," tractor work, road building and ditching, and stump collection for the tar operation.

Spanish Moss on Oak Trees
at R Cattle Ranch at
Murdock, Florida.

Present income on the ranch as now operated is shown thus;- 1948

Cattle	$169,000.00	
Gladiola land	4,000.00	-400 acres leased @ $10.00
Hunting rights	4,000.00	
Oil lease	25,000.00	
Tar	35,000.00	
	$237,000.00	

Taxes:

Charlotte County -Land	$8,039.
Personal	3,210.
Sarasota County -Land	3,807.48
	$15,056.48

Ten man are kept as permanent help on the ranch.

Tractor work road building and ditching will be additional expense and also the cost of collecting stumps for the tar pit operation.

There are about 40,000,000 feet of merchantable timber on the ranch now. There is also a large amount of pulpwood.

TELEPHONE NEptune
Res. 2-3252 Office 2-3259
WESTERN UNION TELEGRAPH
Punta Gorda, Fla

CATTLE - WOOD
AND PINE TAR
FOR SALE

REFERENCES
Punta Gorda State Bank
Punta Gorda, Fla.
Lee County Bank
Fort Myers, Fla.
First National Bank
Fort Myers, Fla.

A. C. FRIZZELL

BREEDER OF

REGISTERED BRAHMAN CATTLE

MURDOCK, FLORIDA

ADVICE FOR OUR EMPLOYEES !!!!!!

1- Don't lie. It wastes my time and yours. I am sure to catch you in the end, and that is the wrong end.

2- Watch your work, not the clock, a long day's work makes a long day short; and a short day's work makes my face long.

3- Give me more than I expect, and I will give you more than you expect. I can afford to increase your pay if you increase my profits.

4- You owe so much to yourself that you cannot afford to owe anybody else. Keep out of debt, or keep out of my work.

5- Dishonesty is never an accident. Good men, like good women, never see temtation when they meet it.

6- Mind your own business, and in time you'll have a business of your own to mind.

7- Don't do anything here which hurts your self-respect. An employee who is willing to steal for me is willing to steal from us.

8- It is none of my business what you do at night, but if dissipating affects what you do the next day, and you do half as much as I demand, you'll last half as long as you hoped.

9- Don't tell me what I'd like to hear, but what I ought to hear. I don't want a valet to my vanity, but one for my money.

10- Don't kick if I kick. If your're worth while correcting, your're worth while keeping. I don't waste time cutting specks out of rotten apples.

See the next page for a more legible rendering of Granddaddy's "advice."

ADVICE FOR OUR EMPLOYEES !!!!!!

1- Don't lie. It wastes my time and yours. I am sure to catch you in the end, and that is the wrong end.

2- Watch your work, not the clock, a long day's work makes a long day short; and a short day's work makes my face long.

3- Give me more than I expect, and I will give you more than you expect. I can afford to increase your pay if you increase my profits.

4- You owe so much to yourself that you cannot afford to owe anybody else. Keep out of debt, or keep out of my work.

5- Dishonesty is never an accident. Good men, like good women, never see temtation when they meet it.

6- Mind you own business, and in time you'll have a business of your own to mind.

7- Don't do anything here which hurts your self-respect. An employee who is willing to steal for me is willing to steal from us.

8- It is none of my business what you do at night, but if dissipating affects what you do the next day, and you do half as much as I demand, you'll last half as long as you hoped.

9- Don't tell me what I'd like to hear, but what I ought to hear. I don't want a valet to my vanity, but one for my money.

10- Don't kick if I kick. If you're worth while correcting, you're worth while keeping. I don't waste time cutting specks out of rotten apples.

Left to right, "Seaboard Airline Railroad Depot, Murdock Store, and [School-Church in front of] Quarter"
On El Jobean Highway 776 looking toward Highway 41.

"Cattle crossing Highway 41 at Murdock.""A. C. with Cherry in front of Mercantile."

On Halloween, Granddaddy's mother, Grandma Blanche, was admitted to Lee Memorial Hospital in Ft. Myers, and Granddaddy's ad for the sale of an El Jobean home appeared in the paper.

> October 31, 1948 **FOR RENT OR SALE**
> 5-room cottage furnished, lights, hot and cold water. Also trailer park adjoining, space for 70 trailers. Located on the Myakka River at El Jobean, Fla. Hard roads, fine fishing. Will rent for $100 per month for five months or sell.
> A. C. FRIZZELL, OWNER

Murdock, Fla. Phone Punta Gorda. L. D. 82

"Cherry with Poon"

The very next day after being admitted to the Ft. Myers hospital, on November 1, 1948, Granddaddy's mother, Grandma Blanche, died after a brief illness. It was three days before her 77th birthday. She was a member of the First Baptist church in Punta Gorda and "active in all the departments, including the Women's Missionary Union and the Sunday School." At her funeral, there were many flowers and a large attendance. She was buried beside her husband, Joseph, in the Frizzell family plot at the Charlotte Harbor Cemetery.

Only a few weeks later, it was Thanksgiving, and Mother, who had hunted with her father in Michigan, brought home the turkey. She honored her pilgrim ancestors, three of whom had arrived on the Mayflower, and she wrote her own story about it.

Their hunting truck on a different hunting trip
(Jack Hindman on top and Daddy in cab).

Mother's Turkey Story

On the day before the opening of hunting season, Paul, our friend Alto, and I drove our Jeep deep into the pine woods of Charlotte County. [Two years later, Alto would marry Uncle Tilley's sister, Amanda, who was 16 years younger than Uncle Tilley.] We drove through palmettos, creeks, and swamps, past Little Salt Springs to a secluded oak hammock, where we watched three wild turkeys feeding on acorns. At sunset, the birds flew up, going to roost for the night on a high limb of a tall pine tree.

We rode home to sleep for a few hours, until Alto returned at 4:00am, when we traveled back into the woods in the frosty darkness, full of anticipation and excitement. Upon our arrival at the same pine tree, we gazed upward and saw, in the glow of the moonlight, the black silhouettes of our three turkeys in a row, still asleep on their roost. What a spectacular sight!

We waited for daylight impatiently and silently, except for low whispers. I selected the middle turkey; Alto chose the one on the left; and Paul chose the one on the right. Alto gave a prearranged hand signal at official sunrise time. I aimed steadily and fired the first shot; my turkey plummeted to earth with a thud, smashing dead branches as it fell. What a thrill! I could hardly believe it! Seconds after my shot, the men fired simultaneously, but their turkeys flew away, flapping their wings loudly.

"Jump in the Jeep!" yelled Alto, as Paul swung into the driver's seat and started the engine in one motion.

I scrambled into my seat, asking, "What about my turkey?"

"No time for that now," replied Paul. "We've got to catch up with our turkeys."

We drove a few hundred yards, spotted them, and stopped. The men shot at them, wounding one. The turkeys disappeared quickly into the dense palmettos.

After a diligent search, Alto said, "Let's go back and get Sandra's turkey."

Paul agreed and drove back to the tall pine tree, found my turkey, and tagged it with one of the turkey tags from my hunting license. The law allowed a limit of one turkey per day and two in a season per hunter.

As we headed for home, we came to a gate where a game warden was waiting. "Let me see your turkeys, fellows," he ordered sternly.

The two men, who were expert skeet marksmen and hunters [probably why Daddy survived World War II], blushed with embarrassment, as Alto replied, "We'll be happy to show the turkey to you, but it is Sandra's turkey; we missed ours."

When the warden examined my wild turkey and exclaimed, "What a fine bird!" I beamed with pleasure. "Could I see your licenses and guns, please?" asked the warden.

As he matched the numbered tag on the turkey to the number on my license, he commented, "I don't believe your story that she shot this bird. I think you brought her along, so you could kill more than your limit, but I can't prove it, so go along home."

The story of my wild turkey spread rapidly throughout the then sparsely-populated county. Although scarcely anyone believed that I shot my turkey, I roasted and served my wild turkey with pride for our family Thanksgiving dinner that year, the same as our pilgrim ancestors had done on the first Thanksgiving more than 300 years ago.

Turkey also appeared on our table for Christmas that year at the annual Christmas banquet and party of the West Coast Scottish Rite club, held in the Masonic Temple in Punta Gorda. It was the first of many that our family would attend. The banquet hall, where we enjoyed a turkey dinner with all the fixings, was beautifully decorated with a Christmas tree in its center and red roses running the length of the banquet tables. After dinner, everybody sang Christmas carols. During the singing of Jingle Bells, Santa Claus made his appearance with gifts and treats for the children.[16]

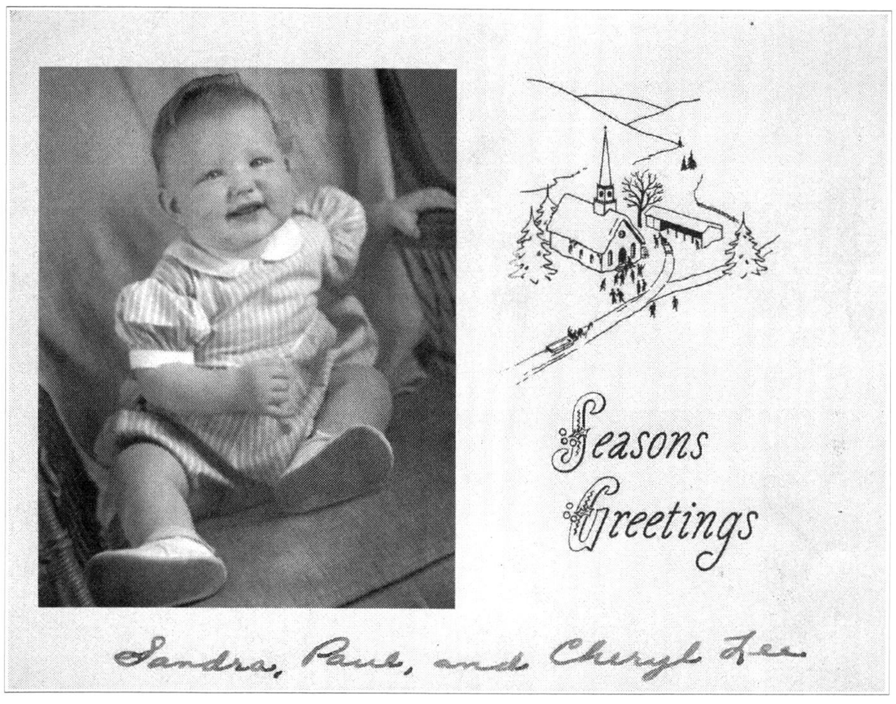

January 1949 was a month with five Sundays, and so Daddy and Mother took me to my first of many Fifth Sunday Sings. They were held on the Fifth Sunday of every month that had one. People gathered from miles around under massive oak trees in the large, grassy yard of an African-American Baptist church that was located way up the Myakka River.

I remember when I was a young girl, sitting on the wooden floor of the rustic church beside a piano bench, while a roly-poly black lady played holy rollin' gospel all over the keyboard. She bounced up and down that bench while she played up and down that keyboard, and I thought she was amazing.

Outside the church, we spread our picnics in the yard under the moss-laden oak trees, and we sang old gospel songs all day long. It is one of my favorite childhood memories.

"Picnic at Myakka City."

In February, five teenage boys robbed the Mercantile of $300 in cash and merchandise from the store and $46.33 from the post office. They then drove to the Florida Keys, where they were captured at a roadblock on the Overseas Highway, after robbing a Tavernier grocery store. They had transported a stolen car across the state line and were suspected of a number of robberies between their home state of Wisconsin and Florida.[17]

In April, Granddaddy took a photographic tour of the ranch. He thought the "cattle still show pretty good."

"Cattle are gentle"

Soon after his tour, he gave Daniel a ride from Charlotte Harbor to Murdock and told him that he had gotten 40,000 pounds of potatoes from the government for stock food. This was from the U. S. Price-Support Program, "by which the article is bought at the 'floor' price when the producer cannot get as much in open market."

Summer 1949 began as all summers had, since 1928, with the annual Arcadia All-Florida Championship Rodeo, and Daddy may have been among those cowboys who performed. According to family lore, he performed at the rodeos, and at his last one, he fell off a bull and injured his back. His back would cause him pain for the rest of his life. Another family story explains that he injured his back when he picked up a big tractor tire and heaved it.

"Arcadia Rodeo June 3, 1949."

That summer, Charlotte County adopted a new seven million dollar tax roll that was almost $300,000 higher than the previous year's. On July 15, Granddaddy was one of three cattlemen and landowners who protested. Represented by his attorney, Leo Wotitzky, he said that his range lands along the highways were excessively valued. His protest was rejected.[18]

On the same day that his protest was rejected, he and Granny left for an "extended" vacation in Georgia and Alabama;[19] while they were visiting our southern relatives, Mother, Daddy, and I were in Michigan visiting our northern ones. Mother was about five months pregnant with my brother Steve, due to be born in November.

By August 3, we were all back in Murdock, when Granddaddy attended a Punta Gorda City Commission meeting. He donated rock and marl for a seawall around the Boy Scout hut on the bayfront.[20]

A couple of weeks later, our summer ended with a Scottish Rite party at a Punta Gorda Beach cottage for a covered dish supper, swimming, and boat riding.[21]

While we were partying at the beach, Daniel Child's summer ended on a much less festive note, when he happened to look across his grove lot and saw the white body of an animal with a swelled belly. He walked over to check it out and saw that it was a Brahma heifer that had been in and out of his place for several weeks.

"She was dead, as of last night, and bloated, but not showing other decomposition."

He walked over to Granddaddy's house and reported the death to him. "He said he would come later."

> Mr. Frizzell came and looked at the calf. We were not able to determine anything as to cause of death. He said he could have her skinned, but did not say he would do so. Idea of my burying body seems the conclusion.
>
> Came in from burying Mr. Frizzell's big Brahma heifer calf in the pasture. Dug over two feet deep, to water, and put a layer of cactus and cow manure in the covering. Took a good sweat digging with shovel and post hole digger.

On September 7, Granddaddy bought another ranch, this one 15,500 acres in Alva, about twenty miles east of Ft. Myers, for $32,500. It was one of Lee County's outstanding cattle spreads. He also bought fifty head of Brahman cattle and 250 other cattle.[22]

Other real estate transactions in 1949 included: the purchase of 160 acres in the LeHigh Acres area and the purchase of 3,250 acres in the McCall area from Seaboard Air Line Railroad Company; the sale of 40 acres in what is now the Punta Gorda Isles area and two Farm Lots in the Gulf Cove area; and the transfer of three El Jobean lots to the First Baptist Church of Charlotte Harbor.

By September, Mother, who had begun immersing herself in Punta Gorda's social life, co-chaired a banquet for the first fall meeting of the Junior Women's Club. Back in the spring, she had been elected first vice president of the club. The theme of the banquet was aptly "Hitch Your Wagon to a Star." During the meeting, she was presented with a gift for winning the club song-writing contest.[23] Of interest is that she was tone-deaf. Perhaps Daddy helped her write the song; he was musically gifted and played the harmonica by ear.

Then on November 6, Granddaddy gave Daniel a ride to Murdock from a Charlotte Harbor church service "in his Deluxe Chrysler four-door sedan," and he told Daniel that he was "getting 100 pounds of a new winter grass from California, said to stand several degrees of frost. He also is clearing palmettos with a new 'whip' rig, which undercuts the saw palmetto."

A week later on November 12, my brother Steve was born in Charlotte Hospital in Punta Gorda.

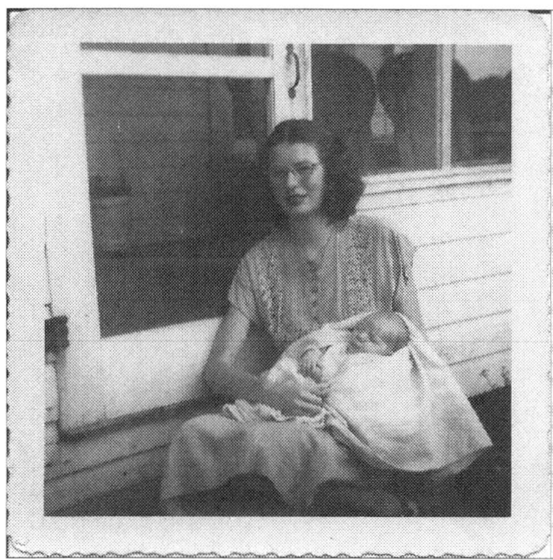

A couple of weeks later, Granddaddy and Uncle Tilley were among six Charlotte County cattlemen who agreed to give a limited number of hunting permits to good sportsmen for hunting in their pastures.[23]

November 30, 1949
LIGHT WOOD
$9 PER CORD
All Good Split
Or Round Wood
A. C. FRIZZELL
F.O.B., MURDOCK, FLA.

December 4, 1949
40 THOUSAND Lighter fence posts 7 ft. long. 1000 or less 26 cents each: 1000 or more, 25 cents each. F.O.B. box cars or truck. Alva, Fla. 11-ft. cowpen post, 70 cents each. Piling cut to order 8 cents per ft.
A. C. Frizzell, Murdock, Fla.

According to Daniel, the following "item" appeared in the December 22, 1949, Herald:

HAS LEG AMPUTATED
Mrs. A. C. Frizzell of Murdock Tuesday (20th) underwent the amputation of a leg in a Wauchula hospital and was reported yesterday still in serious condition.

With Granny seriously suffering from an amputated leg, a dark cloud hung over Daddy for New Year's Eve, when he and Mother joined 100 other guests for the social event of the season at the Hotel Charlotte Harbor. There, they attended their first annual New Year's buffet dinner and ball. The steward chef for the occasion had spent many hours carving elaborate ice sculptures. In a freezing room, he had carved the numbers 1950 from a 300-pound block of ice. He also carved a clock set to the hour and a cupid, both positioned around a large baked ham.[25]

A month later, Daddy and Mother hosted a barbecue rib supper at the monthly meeting of the West Coast Scottish Rite Club at the Masonic Temple in Punta Gorda.[26]

Then the following month, they were initiated into the Order of the Eastern Star at an impressive ceremony at the Masonic Hall. The worthy matron was Uncle Tilley's sister, Amanda. Cookies and fruit punch were served.[27]

Their social life in Punta Gorda had continued growing and their monthly get-togethers now included the Masons, the Eastern Star, the Junior Women's Club, the Charlotte County Democratic Committee, and the Florida Cattlemen's Association. They would both serve as officers in all of the organizations.

While their social life continued growing, Granny's health continued declining. By February, after staying in the hospital for fourteen weeks, she was at home with three nurses caring for her. Her digestive difficulties were so severe that she was obliged to resort to morphine.

As for work on the ranch, it continued as usual. That spring, Granddaddy planted twelve acres of sugar cane for stock feed, while Daddy worked with the cattle, and Mother did the bookkeeping, as well as census enumerating for the year 1950.

Granddaddy's work may have continued as usual, but his troubles grew as fast as his wife's morphine needs and his son's unsolicited social life. Perhaps Granny's leg amputation sent him into a tailspin that resulted in four lawsuits and two drunk driving arrests in only one year beginning that March. For a man like Granddaddy, however, they were mere annoyances. Nothing stopped him; nothing even slowed him down.

In March, Irwin Feher of Georgia filed a $25,000 damage suit against Granddaddy for a car wreck that Feher had with one of Granddaddy's cows on Highway 41, in the area where North Port is today. He charged that Granddaddy had "carelessly and negligently" allowed the cow to roam at large on the highway, and the cow had caused the accident. His left hand had been smashed and lacerated, resulting in permanent injury and weakness, and he had suffered great mental and physical pain.[28]

A month later in April, skies were temporarily blue for Granddaddy when we moved into a house next door to him, and he was pleased. Daniel wrote that Paul "has moved into his new blue roof house and has a sign A. P. FRIZZELL on the front gate post."

Our new house was next door to Granddaddy's and Granny's house on the northwest side. It also faced Highway 41. Our first house had been cold in the winter with the wind blowing through cracks between the boards in the floor and in the walls. It leaked, and it creaked. The second house was much better built and new.

By the time we moved, Granddaddy had added a room for Granny on the right side of their house with a ramp that allowed her wheelchair entry at the back of the house.

Soon after our move, Granddaddy bought the Johnson Lumber Company property in Ft. Myers for $7,500.[29]

Then, the blue skies of April quickly darkened and blew in a nasty front of lawsuits, one in May and one in June.

In May, Jack Whidden filed an $18,000 damage suit against Granddaddy for almost $14,000 owed him for cutting timber, for two trucks with trailers, and for a sawmill without an engine valued at $2,500. The declaration stated that Granddaddy still possessed most of the equipment used by Whidden to cut the timber and that he refused to turn it over or to pay for it.[30]

Then in June, Philip Henry Fortney, a poultry man of Plant City and Hollywood, sued Granddaddy for $25,000 for damages caused on June 23, when Fortney had an automobile accident with Dorothy Carey, who was driving Granddaddy's 1947 Chrysler. Dorothy was Granddaddy's current girlfriend and would later become his second wife after Granny died.

The accident took place on the Tamiami Trail south of Punta Gorda, when Dorothy tried to pass Fortney and knocked his 1949 Plymouth into a canal. As a result, about 600 baby chicks on his back seat drowned, and Fortney injured his back and abdomen and suffered "great pain and shock." Dorothy stopped, but then sped away, and Granddaddy's car was found behind Alligator Bar (the old Acline Wine Place). Fortney was spending large sums of money on medical care and was unable to work. The complaint said that Granddaddy had given Dorothy permission to drive his car, and she was driving it 70 miles per hour "in a negligent and careless manner."

She was arrested after the accident on charges of reckless driving while her license was suspended for a drunken driving conviction. She was released under a $250 cash bond, which she forfeited when she failed to appear in court.[31] Almost a year later, in the circuit court in Punta Gorda, Philip Fortney was awarded $3,500.[32]

Shortly after Dorothy's accident, came the Arcadia annual All-Florida Championship Rodeo. From July 2 to 4, three afternoon performances took place each day that year. A total of $1,500 in prizes, with entry fees, was posted for cowboys competing in bulldogging, bronc riding, bull riding, and calf roping. According to *The Tampa Tribune*, during the July 4th performance, Granddaddy gave away a registered Brahman heifer from his ranch.

A month later on August 11, the Charlotte County Democratic Committee held a reorganization meeting, and full membership showed up to participate. Officers were elected, among them Mother for secretary.[33]

Next day, Granddaddy gave Daniel a ride "in his new four-door Ford sedan." He told Daniel that he "believes in prices being regulated by the law of supply and demand. Thinks we are in for a bad time in the prospective war with Russia."

> August 31, 1950
> West Texas Livestock Weekly
> Vol. 2 – No. 30
> San Angelo, Texas
> **LIVESTOCK FOR SALE** 465 Brahman type cows, bred to good Brahman bulls, $135.00 each. 162 Brahman type cows, with calves at their sides, $185.00 cow and calf. 665 two and three year old Brahman heifers - one half of them are three years old and bred to Brahman bulls, $126.00 per head. 35 Registered Brahman bulls, $300.00 each. The cattle are on the Frizzell Ranch, twelve miles South of Arcadia, Florida.
> Post Office address - A. C. Frizzell Murdock, Florida.

At 2:00am on September 18, Granddaddy was headed south toward Ft. Myers, when he was arrested by a Ft. Myers city cop on the north fill of the Edison Bridge. He was charged with drunk driving and released on $500 bond.

Then on September 29, his attorney appeared in court to argue that the city cop had no jurisdiction to arrest Granddaddy where he did. The judge thought about it overnight and the next day, he ruled that the location was in the cop's jurisdiction as designated by a city limits sign north of there.

The case went on to circuit court where, on November 29, the city of Ft. Myers lost the first round, but on December 18, Granddaddy lost, and a final hearing was set for January 3. On January 3, he appealed it to the State Supreme Court.[34]

That was about ROUND 6. At this point, the case appears to have fallen by the wayside.

Six months after the lawsuit had erupted from Dorothy's accident, yet another person jumped on the lawsuit bandwagon. In the middle of Granddaddy's Supreme Court drunk driving case, on December 6, 1950, P. R. Read, Sr., Arcadia real estate broker, filed suit against Granddaddy for $25,000, alleging that Granddaddy had failed to compensate him when he found a buyer on Granddaddy's terms for his 18,250-acre Alva ranch property. Granddaddy had listed it with Read for $8 per acre and then contracted a sale with an outside party for $9 per acre without Read's knowledge or consent.[35]

The sale was final on December 22 at a purchase price of $136,900, which was $7.50 per acre. At the same time, Granddaddy also sold 600 head of cattle from that ranch and the ranch equipment and machinery for an undisclosed amount.[36]

Almost eight months later, a circuit judge ruled in Granddaddy's favor in the lawsuit. He ruled that Frank Whealton of Tampa had sold the property, and Granddaddy had paid him a commission.[37]

About the same time that Granddaddy closed on the Alva ranch, he bought around 25,000 more acres in the Alva area. The purchase included ten acres plus three very sizable parcels, one for $70,000. Earlier in the year, he had bought scattered tracts there totaling 940 acres plus 840 other acres in three different transactions.

During that year of 1950, while his attorney was running in and out of court with all of the lawsuits, no doubt humoring Granddaddy and at the same time, exacerbating his longstanding feud with law enforcement, Granddaddy had simply continued buying more property. In addition to the Alva property mentioned above, he bought a total of six El Jobean lots, 110 acres next to Murdock, 120 acres in Gulf Cove, and 80 acres on the Peace River on the south side of Charlotte Harbor. How did he keep track of it all?

For Christmas 1950, Daddy and Mother took Steve and me to the annual Scottish Rite Club supper and yule party at the Masonic Lodge. Joyce Hindman, President, was general manager, and Daddy was secretary and treasurer. The room was decorated with holly, and the lighted Christmas tree with candles, toys, and other gifts that Santa distributed.[38]

Daniel wrote that the Frizzell men gave him their usual Christmas gift of two or three pounds of fresh beef.

A. C. FRIZZELL
Announces
Effective January 1, 1951
The Management of his
Cattle Ranch at Murdock
in the hands of son
Paul Frizzell

In January, Granny moved into Wauchula Hospital, where she would live for the next year, while life continued as usual for Granddaddy. During the days, he continued buying land here and there and everywhere. He exhibited at the county fair, was arrested for drunk driving, toured El Jobean with Daniel, attended a cattlemen's fish fry, bought some illegal wild quail, planted forty acres of grass per day, visited Granny in the hospital, and conducted cattle business with the Vanderbilts. In the evenings, he hung his hat at the Alligator Bar (the old Acline Wine Place), where his girlfriend, Dorothy, worked.

He first bought "all the remainder of El Jobean" that was in Joel Bean's Trust. The purchase included an area east of the village called Myakka Country Club Golf Course, which never materialized.

A couple of weeks later, he made quite a showing at the Charlotte County Fair in Punta Gorda. During the fair's cattle show in the morning, he exhibited the top Charollais bull, and in the Devon division, he showed the best cow and calf. Uncle Tilley exhibited the best Brahman bull and female.[39]

Daniel wrote about attending the fair. He said that the admission was twenty-five cents, and coffee at the Methodist booth cost ten cents. He added that Granddaddy had the biggest Brahma bull at 2,200 pounds.

In February, Granddaddy was arrested again for driving while intoxicated, this time on the Tamiami Trail near Venice at 11pm.[40]

A couple of months later, he took Daniel to visit the El Jobean Mission on Palm Sunday. "Besides seeing the wonderful pasture development of A. C. F. and town enlargement and beautification of El Jobean, heard wonderful story of soaring cattle (calf) prices, where four medium-grade Holsteins brought over $200 each."

March 31, 1951, Daniel's diary:

ROUNDUP AT FRIZZELL PENS

Daddy and Granddaddy "at the Cowpens."

My brother, Steve, talked to me about roundup one day. He said that when he was a little boy, Daddy would take him to roundup. Roundup was once a year every spring. The purpose of roundup was to find all the calves, brand them, dip them, and castrate them.

He said the cowboys would grab the calves, throw them on the ground, tie their feet, and brand them with a hot iron from a fire. The sons of the black workers would watch and go in with the calves. They would grab one around the neck and twist its head until it fell to the ground. It was called throwing the calf.

One day when Steve was watching, Daddy told him to do it. Steve grabbed one of the calves around the neck, but it dragged him around and around the pen, and he held on for dear life. After that, Daddy gave up on the idea of Steve throwing calves.

Steve also remembers watching the cattle go down the dip chute and drop into the vat all the way under. As for castration, a lot of bulls were not needed, and steers would grow to be better meat producers, instead of tough ol' bulls.

One evening during roundup that year, Granddaddy took a break and attended a monthly meeting of the Charlotte County Cattlemen's Association at the city waterworks dam at Shell Creek. A fish fry included grits, hush puppies, slaw, pickles, and coffee.[41]

A couple of weeks later, Daniel "saw Paul Frizzell, who was driving the Jeep."

"FIRE IN THE HOLE"

Granddaddy's troubles did not end with his previous four lawsuits and two drunk driving arrests. Early in May, with his usual total disregard for the law, he bought twenty-three illegal wild quail from W. E. Croy, who was a state wildlife officer, and they got caught when another wildlife officer filed a charge against Croy. Croy had to resign his job after pleading guilty to the charge.[42] Three years before, Croy had worked in the Mercantile for a short time.

On June 15 that year, my brother Alan Claire "A. C." was born at Charlotte Hospital in Punta Gorda.

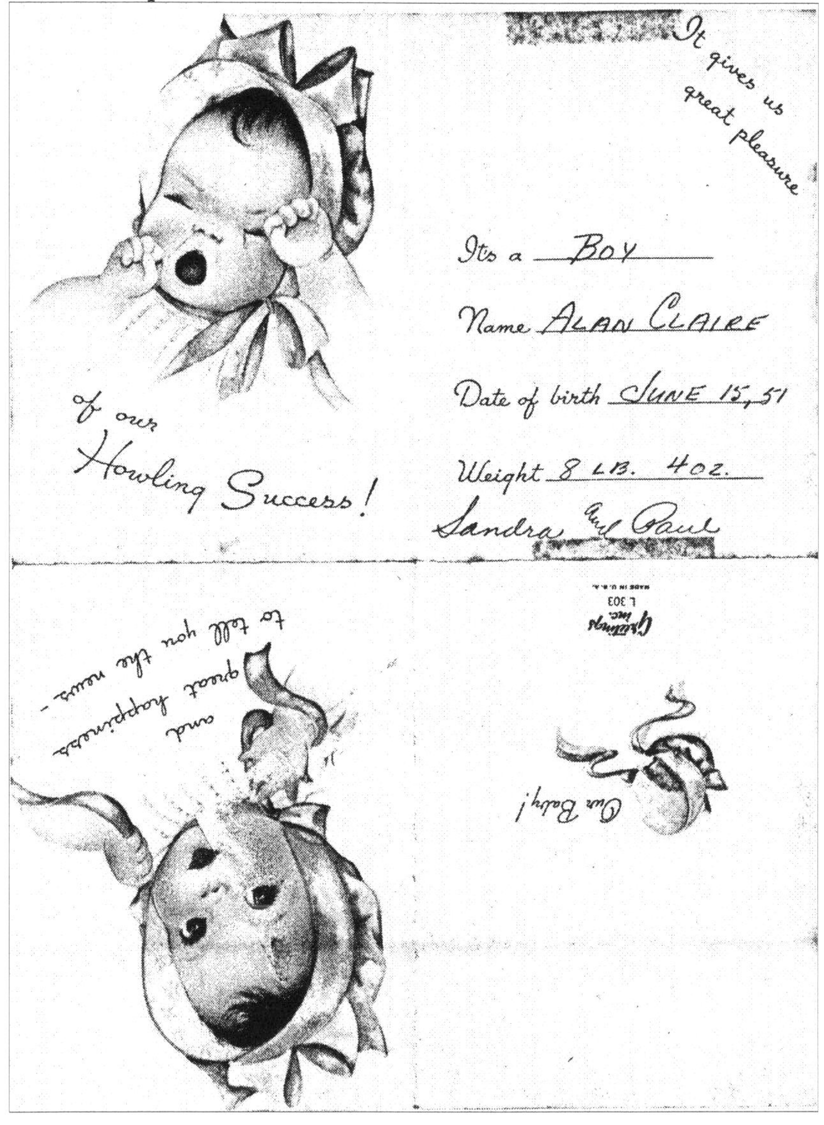

On the day that A. C. was born, Granddaddy bought forty acres in Gulf Cove; then in July, he bought eighty more acres in Gulf Cove and a tract in El Jobean Garden Truck; and in August, he bought four lots in Charlotte Harbor.

When he was not buying land that summer, he was planting about forty acres daily of pangola grass, while Granny was living at the Wauchula Hospital, where she had two nurses and regular nightly visits by a doctor. She had been there for six months.

> July 2, 1951
> HOUSEKEEPER
> Middle-age, to live in: care for children.
> Telephone LD 82-1, collect.
> PAUL FRIZZELL, AP Cattle Ranch, Murdock, Fla.

Early in the morning on September 23, a strange event took place at one of Granddaddy's sawmills. Three black men in a car with a Pinellas County tag approached Charles Warner, the manager of the sawmill, which was located a couple of miles north of Punta Gorda. They asked permission to "dig for money" in one of the abandoned sawdust piles. They said the money had been hidden there by a friend who was later deported to Cuba, and they promised Warner a share of whatever they found.

Warner got approval from Granddaddy, and the men started digging. After about two hours spent digging in the damp sawdust pile and probing it with a sharp stick, they told Warner that they had found nothing, then they hurried to get in their car, and they sped away. Warner reported the incident to Sheriff Quednau who investigated and found an empty ladies' handbag on the ground nearby that had obviously been removed from the damp sawdust pile.[43]

That fall, Granddaddy went on another of his buying sprees. In September, he bought a parcel in Gulf Cove for $3,840 and two lots in Punta Gorda. Then in October, he bought two lots in the McCall area on the river and about thirty-five lots in El Jobean with frontage on the imaginary golf course that he had bought there in January. In November, he bought more than 300 acres from a Roman Catholic Bishop of Louisville, Kentucky, all along the Myakka River across from El Jobean in the McCall area on the way to Placida.

Granddaddy may have accomplished in one month what others might accomplish in one year, but he always made time for his family.

He loved us with the same intensity that motivated him in everything that he did.

On November 14 that year, Daddy went with Jack Hindman and Uncle Tillie to Clewiston for the annual Florida State Cattlemen's Association meeting. They represented the Charlotte County Cattlemen's Association.[44] The meeting was designed for the instruction and enjoyment of its members.

A month later, along came two Vanderbilt brothers, one a former governor of Rhode Island and owner of a registered dairy herd in Massachusetts. During the week of December 15, the two brothers paid $700,700 for 35,000 acres of Cape Haze land adjacent to Granddaddy's ranch, between the ranch and Englewood. The land would later be known as Rotonda. They planned to buy a few cattle from Granddaddy and to develop their wild land into a cattle ranch called the Two-V Ranch. They would plant grass, build a ranch house and construct roads. Their land was land that Granddaddy's cattle had roamed for many years, and he had leased it at one time for grazing.[45]

A year later, the Orlando Sentinel reported on the considerable progress that the Vanderbilts had made improving pasture on their new ranch. They were leasing to Granddaddy 20,000 grazing acres of the 35,000 acres that they owned. They had bought their first cattle from Granddaddy, 850 mixed half to three quarters Brahmans that they were breeding with registered Brahman bulls from another herd, and they had bought a registered Santa Gertrudis herd.[46]

Next door to them, Granddaddy's cattle continued grazing on a couple hundred thousand acres of land and often claimed the right-of-way on Highway 41, as did his cowboys on their horses, while a steady flow of cattle trucks cluttered the traffic there. Highway 41 was a multi-use highway in Murdock, with automobiles, of necessity, yielding to all others.

Thirty years before, Granddaddy had volunteered mules and crews to help build Highway 41 through Charlotte County. Did he ever imagine of what value it would be to him in the future? Yes.

On January 7 in the new year of 1952, Daniel "noted activity at the Frizzell corral and two trucks of cattle northbound. About eight mounted cowboys were on the highway after the trucks left."

Four of the cowboys on Highway 41.

Granddaddy's cattle and cowboys were not the only ones traveling along Highway 41. Peddlers in covered wagons pulled by mules occasionally passed through the ranch. They sold just about anything anyone could want. They were a mercantile on wheels.

One day, one came by with the words, "THE OLD WEST STILL LIVES," painted on the wagon's canvas. Two mules pulled the wagon. A goat stood atop one mule, and a dog stood on the other. The peddler did not sit on a wagon bench to drive the mules; he stood on a platform directly behind the mules.

From January 13 to 19, the Third Annual Charlotte County Fair exhibited manufactured and agricultural products with emphasis on Florida's cattle industry. Granddaddy was, again, among those who were awarded livestock prizes.[47]

> January 24, 1952
> WANT young married man to run and manage general country store and gas station. Long hours. Must furn. reference. A. C. Frizzell, Murdock, Fla.

A couple of weeks later, Granddaddy was featured in "Cattle Clatter" in the Orlando Sentinel. The article discussed his extensive pasture improvement operations. He was running four or five tractors, a bulldozer, and a Webb plow. [The Webb plow, designed in 1917 by Henry C. Webb, an African-American man from Bradenton, was used for cutting out palmetto roots.] "Last year, he set out 1,000 acres of Pangola, 500 of Torpedo, 250 of Pensacola, and 250 of Common Bahia. And he hopes to increase acreage this year by several thousand acres." He said he was doing it because he did not have enough grass for his cattle.[48]

By now, Daddy was president of the Charlotte County Cattlemen's Association, and in April, he and Jack Hindman attended a call meeting at the county agent's office to discuss cattle inspection laws.[49]

Then in May, Granddaddy gave Daniel a ride to the Charlotte Harbor Baptist Church. "He and his young colored driver were on their way to visit Miss Pattie at Wauchula, where they now have a house for her, so she can live near the hospital, have a regular nurse, yet be 'at home.'"

> May 31, 1952
> FOR SALE: TD 18 Crawler Tractor without bulldozer.
> Will need some repairs. Price $2300.
> A. C. Frizzell, Murdock, Fla.

On June 23, Granddaddy made a deal at the Debson Ranch east of Punta Gorda to buy the trees, except for two acres surrounding Hunters Camp on Shell Creek. He agreed to cut all the Southern

Yellow Pine Trees marked by the seller, which would be all trees eight inches in diameter and up. He agreed to pay $18 per 1000 mill run, with $5,000 down and $5,000 one month later. He guaranteed a monthly run of 140,000 to 150,000 board feet and would pay on the 10th of each month. The agreement was in effect for three years.

Two days later, an article in the *Ft. Myers News-Press* talked about how Daddy had recently finished "25 miles of shallow surface ditches connecting a network of ponds together to give a gradual but steady surface water relief from a vast water-shed in the north of his pasture."[50]

A previous article two months earlier had discussed how Daddy had started the surface water control plan the first of the year [which meant that he had averaged about four miles of ditch per month, or about one mile per week]. It explained, "These ditches average less than a foot deep and are for surface water relief and not canal drainage. Waterways engineers believe that these ditches will halve the days the flatwoods are underwater." Other farmers and ranchers are doing the same.[51]

On August 11, Governor Fuller Warren sent a telegram to Daddy, appointing him to the State Livestock Sanitary Board. At the time, Daddy was still President of the Charlotte County Cattlemen's Association. The purpose of the livestock sanitary board was to control cattle diseases. Members served for four years and received no salaries, but were given expenses.

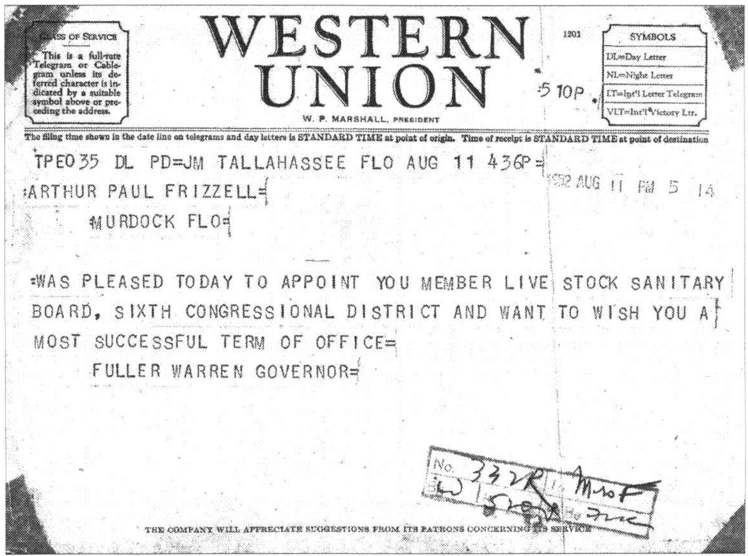

WESTERN UNION

W. P. MARSHALL, PRESIDENT

TPE035 DL PD=JM TALLAHASSEE FLO AUG 11 436P=

ARTHUR PAUL FRIZZELL=
MURDOCK FLO=

WAS PLEASED TODAY TO APPOINT YOU MEMBER LIVE STOCK SANITARY BOARD, SIXTH CONGRESSIONAL DISTRICT AND WANT TO WISH YOU A MOST SUCCESSFUL TERM OF OFFICE=
FULLER WARREN GOVERNOR=

On September 9 at 4:00pm, all members of the Charlotte County Cattlemen's Association met at the Frizzell store at Murdock for a pasture tour of Granddaddy's ranch. After the tour, they hosted supper at Granddaddy's home.[52] Perhaps, the two cows in the below photo graced the grill of the barbecue pit for the occasion.

Butchering two cows on the ranch.
(Daddy on the left and Jack Hindman in the center are watching).

In that same month of September, Granddaddy bought the two-story Bishop residence on Marion Avenue in Punta Gorda. He was the highest of five active bidders at a public auction attended by about forty people. He paid $8,700 for the residence and furnishings that were valued at $7,147.[53]

For Halloween that year, Daddy and Mother attended a costume ball at the Community Hall on October 28. They were among those wearing "outstanding costumes." They wore long night clothes. The Junior Women's Club sponsored the ball, and a large crowd attended.[54]

The next day, Mother, who was seven months pregnant with my sister, Merry, was admitted to Lee Memorial Hospital for an overnight stay.[55]

In November, Granddaddy bought a BIG, new bulldozer. Daniel saw it in front, waiting to be unloaded.

> November 30, 1952
> WANTED, cook and general housekeeper. Modern conveniences. Private room, board, $20 weekly. Write Paul Frizzell, Frizzell Cattle Ranch, Murdock, Florida.

In December, Granddaddy signed an Oil, Gas, and Mineral lease with Sinclair Oil and Gas Company for 4,000+ acres for ten years. He was to receive an annual payment of $2,132.65 plus the usual royalties in the amount of 1/8 for gas, 1/8 for oil, and 1/10 for minerals.

Granddaddy had not transacted any big real estate deals in 1952, but he did transact enough little ones to keep himself busy. He bought over 100 lots and sold about 20 in El Jobean, Punta Gorda, Gulf Cove, and Ft. Myers, and he bought over 1,600 acres in the Gulf Cove and El Jobean areas.

The new year 1953 started with the birth of my sister, Merry Sandra, on January 3 in Lee Memorial Hospital.

A. P. FRIZZELL
BREEDER OF
REGISTERED BRAHMAN CATTLE
Telephone LD821
MURDOCK, FLORIDA

CERTIFICATE
of Entry in the Herd Register

Name Merry Sandra
Holding Brand Frizzell
Private Herd No. 4
Description Light brown hair
Weight 7 pounds 13 ounces
Born January 3rd, 1953
Sire Paul
Dam Sandra

The day after Merry was born, *The Tampa Tribune* reported that records of the Production and Marketing Administration of the U. S. Department of Agriculture at Gainesville revealed that Florida has eleven landowners holding more than 100,000 acres. The biggest was the federal government with several million acres, including one million in the Everglades. Behind the Lykes Brothers and the Duponts, Granddaddy was listed with 130,020 acres, all in graze, except for 400 as cropland.[56]

A month later, *The Tampa Tribune* reported that a Wauchula businessman named Gene Stewart was introducing pheasants to South Florida and breeding them for sale and release in the woods as big game birds. He said that so far Granddaddy was the only South Florida landowner to buy large numbers of his ring-neck pheasants and release them in the woods. He bought about 600 at $2.00 each and released them on his ranch with the plan of having "good shooting in a year or two."[57]

Then on March 5, Granddaddy bought Gibbons Lumber Yard in Punta Gorda for $60,000.[58] It would be a convenient place to sell all the lumber he was cutting from the trees on the nearby Debson Ranch. His agreement to cut trees there was good for two more years.

On that same day, Daniel saw "a big bunch of A. C. cattle, with calves, dogs, and a big force of mounted cowboys pass on the highway with heavy, heavy traffic."

A couple of weeks later, Granddaddy paid $1,050 for the highest price bull at an auction that closed the fourth annual Imperial Eastern Brahman show that took place at the Mid-State Pavillion in Bartow. [59]

And then in May, the DeSoto County commissioners awarded him a contract for a "considerable footage of bridge lumber."[60]

The photo on the next page shows Granddaddy taking time out to visit with his sister, Lula, and her daughter Marijo with her only child John Irvin Brown. Steve remembers that Irvin had diabetes as a child and committed suicide in 2000 at the age of 48, because his health had deteriorated, and he was suffering from the side effects of the disease. His mother, Marijo, would die eight years later in 2008 at the age of 81. The mother and son are buried side by side in Royal Palm Memorial Gardens in Punta Gorda. They share a grave marker.

On May 24, 1953, Granny died at age 82 in the Palmetto Clinic of Wauchula, after spending five days there. She had suffered from coronary heart disease for fifteen years. She was a member of the Methodist Church and Eastern Star of Punta Gorda. Her funeral service was at 2:30pm on May 26 at the First Methodist Church in Wauchula.

She was buried at Wauchula Cemetery, where Granddaddy had bought eight lots for $5 each. In 2015, lots there were selling for $600 each. Beside Granny, would later be buried her daughter, Annabel, and husband, Buster Mathis, and Annabel's daughter, Martha Pearle, and husband, George Vogt. And there they all rest in peace, the three generations, "of true southern ladies," among the last of a dying breed.

Granddaddy in the center wearing his white Stetson hat.

CARD OF THANKS

We wish to extend our sincere and heartfelt thanks to our friends and relatives for their kindness, the many beautiful flowers, sympathy cards and words of condolence extended to us during the illness and death of our loved one, Mrs. Pattie B. Frizzell. We appreciate everything more than words can express.

A. C. Frizzell

Mr. and Mrs. Paul Frizzell and Family.

Mr. and Mrs. Lemuel B. Standifer and Family.

Mr. and Mrs. Buster Mathis and Family.

61

The following Sunday, Daniel rode home from the Charlotte Harbor church with a neighbor. "We talked about Miss Pattie and her funeral at Wauchula, also other events where she was a leading character." He fondly remembered the woman he had known for thirty-five years, a neighbor, a friend, a leader in the community and in the church, an all-around active member of society, and an outstanding woman in her time.

Within a week after the funeral, the new Governor Dan McCarty removed Daddy and the seven other State Livestock Sanitary Board members. Every one of them had been appointed by the previous governor, Fuller Warren. Their functioning as a board had been controversial, and the Florida Cattlemen's Association agreed that they had been a hindrance to the progress of the industry in Florida.[62]

> July 5, 1953
> 1 NEW D8 Caterpillar Tractor, with bulldozer, never been used.
> A. C. Frizzell, Murdock, Fla.

On July 19, Granddaddy started a $6,000 warehouse and display room for a tractor sales and service addition to Frizzell Lumber Company in Ft. Myers.[63]

A week later at the Livestock Pavillion in Bartow, he was named a permanent member of the board of directors of the new Cattle Producers Price Support Association organized by Florida ranchers with the aim of boosting cattle prices.[64]

A couple of months later in September, Uncle Forney moved back to Florida without his wife Annie and started working for Granddaddy at his new lumber yard in Punta Gorda. Uncle Forney and Annie must have separated; the month before, the two of them had deeded to Uncle Forney alone a triangle of property they both owned in Punta Gorda.

The next month on October 9, Hurricane Hazel hit Charlotte Harbor with 85-mile-per-hour winds. In Punta Gorda, roofs ripped off a few buildings, and a few small boats sank, but overall there was not much damage. North of Punta Gorda, however, Highway 41 went about two feet under water and thousands of acres of Granddaddy's ranch flooded on both sides. The water stood so long that the soggy grass lost the nutrients necessary for cattle to maintain their summer weight gains.

A couple of weeks later, Daddy, who was now state director for the Cattlemen's Association, went with nine other Florida cattlemen to Washington, D. C., to meet with the Secretary of Agriculture. The Cattle Producers Support Association had sent two resolutions to the secretary more than three months before and received no response.[65]

The Florida cattlemen joined others from all over the country to try to get aid in the form of a federal subsidy for their industry. While Midwest pastures were suffering from drought, Florida pastures were under water from torrential autumn rains. Thirty-one counties had been declared disaster areas by Eisenhower the week before. The cattlemen were looking for permanent aid, however, not just emergency relief. Florida ranked 13th in the U. S. in number of cattle and was moving up to 9th. It was considered a grower state for cattle that were then sent to Texas for fattening and to Kansas for market.[66]

On November 9, Granddaddy and Jack Hindman dba Frizzell and Hindman signed two grazing leases with Game and Fresh Water Fish Commission, one for nine years to graze and run cattle on a 15,000-acre pasture for $2,436 per year, and the other for three years on an 11,000-acre pasture for $1,563 per year.

The next year in 1953, Granddaddy would not add much to his holdings. If anything, he lessened them slightly. He only bought about eighty-two lots and fifteen acres, while he sold about seventy-five lots and 450 acres. The properties were located all over Charlotte County and in Ft. Myers.

The year 1953 climaxed with a pre-Thanksgiving outing on the ranch, when Granddaddy sponsored a hunt for four U. S. generals, several aids, and a few of their civilian friends. They were Gen. Nathan F. Twining, chief of staff U. S. Air Force; Gen. Charles Loucks, deputy chief of chemical warfare; Gen. "Flap" Adams, who was Gen. Marshall's executive officer during World War II; and Maj. Gen. Sory Smith, chief of public information U. S. Air Force. Accompanying them were General Adams' wife and friends. They bagged forty-five quail.

After the hunt, they went on a fishing trip in Englewood and caught 146 mackerel, 12 black grouper, 10 kingfish, and 3 blues; back on dry land, they participated in a turkey shoot sponsored by the Englewood Fire Department, and they each got a turkey.[68]

On Pearl Harbor Day, December 7, 1953, only six months after Granny died, Grandma Claire died at the age of 51 in Homestead, Florida; she was buried at Palm Memorial Park in Naranja, Florida.

Sometime in 1949, the Claires had moved their trailer from the Punta Gorda Municipal Trailer Park to the Royal Palm Trailer Park in Homestead. Grandma had taught school at the Charlotte Harbor School and after they moved to Homestead, she taught special education at the Homestead Junior High School. She was too young to die; her children Earl and Carol were only twelve and nine years old respectively.

But the story of the Claires is another book and certainly worthy of one.

END OF AN ERA

One day there will be a house for every cow.

Some say that Granny's death marked the beginning of the end of an era. Perhaps her death put the wheels in motion, but the actual end probably began when we moved to Punta Gorda. Everything seemed OK before we moved, except for Mother. She was very unhappy living in Murdock.

She had insisted on the move to Punta Gorda. She wanted to be more active in her Punta Gorda social life. She wanted us closer to school; I had started first grade, and the others would follow year after year. But most of all, she wanted to get away from Granddaddy's control. She did not like living under his thumb, and so we moved to Punta Gorda, and Daddy left the ranch that he had known and loved for most of his life.

On December 16, 1953, Granddaddy signed an agreement with Daddy to sell a house to him at 508 W. Olympia Avenue in Punta Gorda, and we moved there to live. Granddaddy later called it a "fool" move.

The price was $8,000, payable at the rate of $500 every six months at six percent interest. If Daddy did not make the payments, then whatever payments he had made would be considered rent. It was a three-bedroom, one-bath house, but another bedroom was added in the back of the house behind the kitchen for me.

508 W. Olympia Avenue, Punta Gorda, FL,
on the corner of Olympia and Gill streets,
where the Methodist church campus is today.

When we moved away from the ranch, something tragic and sad happened between Daddy and Granddaddy. Something happened to all of us, but especially to Daddy. We watched him fall into a dark alcoholic abyss from which he would never return. And something happened to Mother. We watched her fall into a rage.

What we did not watch was the agonizing struggle of a great man facing the dilemma of perpetuating or forsaking the empire that he had spent his entire lifetime building. The woman with whom he had built the empire had died six months before, and his only son was disappearing into a bottle of booze. The more he thought about it, the more he saw his legacy fading into oblivion.

Behind closed doors, he struggled with the most crucial and painful decision of his life during that first six months after we moved, but he continued with business as usual, here and there and everywhere.

On January 20 of the new year 1954, the Venice Area Chamber of Commerce announced that Granddaddy and four others had donated land on which to build seventeen miles of road between Venice and the DeSoto County line. The road would connect with a DeSoto County road twenty-three miles long that would lead to Arcadia. When finished, it would open a large area to development that was previously inaccessible.[1]

Two days later, Granddaddy won two firsts at the Charlotte County Fair cattle show, one for Brahman bull over two years old and the other for Brahman cow over two years old. He won a second for heifer between one and two.[2]

> March 20, 1954
> SOMEONE stole eleven Fenton Feeders out of our pastures along U. S. 41 and the Myakka River. Anyone furnishing evidence that leads to the arrest and conviction of the guilty parties will receive a $250 reward.
> A. C. FRIZZELL, MURDOCK, FLA.
> [Fenton Feeders were designed by Carl Fenton of Arcadia. They were cattle feeders that also functioned as windmills.]

In March, Granddaddy paid Lemuel, Annabel, and Daddy $1,000 each for the release of all claims on the estate of their deceased mother, Pattie B. Frizzell, "from the beginning of the world to the day of the date of these presents."

At the same time, The Punta Gorda City Council awarded Granddaddy a contract to provide the city with a new rotary power mower for $300 plus a trade for an old mower.[3] Three months later, it would vote to give him an $825 tax credit in exchange for a used pickup truck.[4]

The next month in May, Daddy revoked the Power of Attorney he had given Granddaddy before he went to war.

Then on June 12, while we were vacationing at our Grandpa Claire's cabin on a lake in Michigan, Granddaddy wrote the following letter. I have paraphrased and paragraphed it for easier reading.

> Dear Paul, Sandra, and all the kids,
> I got your letter, and I note all you have to say, and that you have just begun to think. Well, that is all I do is just think.
>
> Now, Paul, as for me turning over to you to relieve me, and you to run the ranch, that answer is No. First, because I owe $850,000. Now, I know that I can run it better than anyone else. Don't you think so? I have proven what I can do, and the bankers who have loaned me this money know this. I have run bigger things than I am running and made the money to buy these things here at Murdock. I don't suppose you take credit for having made any of these things, do you?
>
> Let's remember this one thing. To get promoted, anyone must work up to and show that he is entitled to a promotion.
>
> Now, let's see what you have done when you wouldn't go to school to apply yourself for something. When I said to you, if you would take a business course in

bookkeeping and typing, I meant by that, before you quit school, to apply yourself so that you could be able to handle all of my books in a manner when the auditors come that we would have things in good shape and know what we were doing. Did you do it? No.

Well, the next best thing I thought was to put you where you would have to meet and do business with the public and, at the same time, make a success, so I decided to put you in the store. You may think that is no place to get experience, but that is where I got my first experience, and I will never forget it, and it did me a lot of good, and I know a hundred people who have made a success in life started in the Mercantile Business.

Now let's see. I put you in the store after you had gone to school about three months. I knew by experience that you could not keep a set of books, but what you had learned would do you a lot of good. It would at least give you some knowledge of bookkeeping when you saw it, a DR and a CR.

Did your experience in the store give you the right for a promotion? I don't think so. How about the Ford Place? I don't think so.

Well, I thought, being that you and Sandra were going to get at least 75 percent of what I had worked for, and still am, all of my life, that you would come and not take over the ranch, but carry out my instructions until we at least got it out of debt, but you don't want to do that.

A lot of my mistakes have been caused from listening to others. One was when Doc McQueen kept after me, until I spent $48,000 on Jack Hindman and hired him as a cow foreman. That is why he left, because he wanted to run the ranch, and I would not let him.

This is the same reason I am not going to turn the ranch over to you. If I did not care anything for you, Sandra, and the kids, I would do it. Some smart aleck would be waiting to tear you to pieces, John Hathaway for one. All this mess come up here Christmas was all uncalled for, just by someone meddling in, where they have no business.

Moving away from Murdock was one of the biggest fool things I ever heard of. As for the room on the house, it would have been built, too, long ago. I told you I would get it, and I always do what I say.

I told you if you had wanted me to let you run the ranch, it would have been to have carried out my orders, which you did not do. When I asked you why you had not done these things, you would tell me, "I don't know."

How would you like to have someone that you had working for you, and you would ask him, sometimes a week or ten days later, and he would say, "I don't know." Especially when you were paying him $500.00 every four weeks, hospital insurance at least four or five different companies, also $35,000 life insurance carried and paid on you, so if something happened to you, your family and kids would be protected. All this, and no house rent to pay.

Then, for someone like the bookkeeper, who is not going to get a thing, only his salary, just trying to help, he sent you word about something, and you sent him word back to kiss your ___. What would you think, if you were the bookkeeper, and you were just trying to help, and the man's son sent you back word like that? You would not try to cooperate anymore, would you? Then you said somewhere to someone, one of the first things you would do is to run him off. I have told you myself that Bailey sometimes talked too much trying to help, but I have corrected a lot of this. I am going to say to you that Bailey is one of the best men for me in the place. He isn't trying to take a thing off of me and he is above board, he is honest.

One other thing, he called Sandra, something about getting a hold of you for something. I can't recall. Sandra told him not to call here, that she did not want to be bothered. With all the times she calls Murdock wanting something, I will assure you, she did not get no such answer as that, and she won't.
Well, I will change the subject.

At this point, he talks about work, including cleaning rocks out of a canal, taking a couple dams out, finishing a road and ditches, and putting in miles of canals and ditches all over the place, by the little Flowing Well, down below the Negro Grave Yard, back up in Ringling, and up from Horse Lot, just to mention a few.

Now, Paul, it's up to you and Sandra, what you do, if you come back, both of you, and be the same each week, not so friendly with everybody one week and snoot them the next week. Then, you and I agree on what we are going to do, and you do it, and let me know right along, from time to time, that you have done it. Then, come back. If you don't feel you can do that, then if I were you, I wouldn't come back.

You know, I wanted you to wait until about the middle of July or the first of August, then go to some place where you could relax, and that would have done you

> all good. This way, you haven't had a vacation, but if you think you can do better for yourself, and you all would be better satisfied, then I think that is what you should do.
>
> I am going to say that I am going to fix my estate where you and family will get, each six of you, more than 50 percent of the earnings, which to my way of thinking would be a nice income for each of you. One paragraph is, should you and Sandra separate, that one-sixth goes to you, which you will leave to your heirs, but you all must think it over and settle this question, and if you do come back, then come back with a different attitude, for after all, if I were only thinking of myself, I would bail out in the next 90 days, pay up what I owe, and I would have enough for me to live on.

At this point, he talks about possible deals to sell the ranch, one with an Alco Aluminum man for a big dairy business for Miami, Tampa, and St. Pete, and the other a deal he knows he can make with Maule Industries.

> Well, I will close and go to the store. It is now 9 a. m., and today is pay day.
>
> Dad
>
> P. S. I have bought fertilizer and will start putting it on next week. I hope you are all getting along fine. I expect to leave for Miami, Monday noon and will be down there for two days.

Twelve days later on June 24, he wrote another letter, in which he announced the sale of the ranch. I paraphrased and paragraphed it for easier reading.

Dear Paul, Sandra, and all other 4,
Got your card thanks.
Well, you said you were going to the doctor to see if he could put his finger on what is the matter with you. Well, that you can do more than anyone else yourself, if you make up your mind to do so. There is nothing the matter with you that you can't straighten out yourself, and until you make up your mind to do it yourself, you will be just like this.

By now, Daddy's drinking was completely out of control. Our lives were defined by binge nightmares. Car wrecks, lengthy disappearances, police escorts knocking on the front door, Mother screaming and yelling, awkward and unpredictable situations and special occasions, an element of danger, an element of fear, and lots of worry.

To begin with, if you had told me that if you could just go somewhere here in Florida to be quiet and rest for ten days, I would have believed you meant it, and I could believe it would do you some good, but when you wanted to light out on about a 4,000 mile trip, and on the road all the time, I could not see it.

I expect to take a vacation for ten days about August 1st, but it will be on the beach somewhere here, where I can be rested when I get back and can be got by phone when they want me.

We are still going with all machines. I think I can finish in two weeks. Then, I am bringing everything in, clean it up, and paint it, some repair. Then, I am going to see if I can get some job for it and the men with some road contractor. If can't, I will lay them off.

Well, Paul, I have sold the ranch to Mall [Maule]. It will take 90 days to close the deal. I am to have four years to use it, before I turn it over to them.

TELEPHONE LD 82
WESTERN UNION TELEGRAPH
Punta Gorda, Fla.

CATTLE - WOOD
AND PINE TAR
FOR SALE

REFERENCES
Punta Gorda State Bank
Punta Gorda, Fla.
Lee County Bank
Fort Myers, Fla.
First National Bank
Fort Myers, Fla.

A. C. FRIZZELL

BREEDER OF

REGISTERED BRAHMAN CATTLE

MURDOCK, FLORIDA 6/12/54

Dear Paul Sandra and all the kids
I got your letter and note all you have to say,and that you have just begin to think well that is all I do is just think,Now Paul as for me Turning over to you to Releave me and you to Run the Ranch,that Answer is Now, Fist because I Owe $8 Eight Hundred and Fifty Thousands Dollars Now I know that I can Run it best Better than any one Elce dont you think so I haveProven what I can do and the Bankers who as loandd me this money knows this I have run Bigger things than I am Runing and made the Money to Buy thes things here at Murdock, I dont supose you taak Credit for having Made any of thes things do you less Remember this one thing to get Permoated, any one Must Work upto and show that he is Intitle to a permotion,Now les see what you have doen when you wouldent go to School to aply your self ,for something than I said to you if you would takeabusiness course in book keeping and Tiping, I ment by that to apply youself to be abae to befor you Quit School so that you could be able to handle all of my books in a Maner when the Auditors Come that we would have thing s in good Sape and Know What we Were Doing Did you do it No,well the Next best thing I thought was to Put you where you would have to Meet and do Business with the Publicand and at the same time Make a Success,so I desided to Put you in the Store MouMay think that is No Place to get Experiance but that is where I Got My Fisst Expieranc and I never will forget it and it done me a Lot of Good and I know Hunderd of People who has Made a Successin Life Started in Mercantile BusinessNow less see Now I put you in theStore after you went to school about 3 Mont sI Knew by Experiance that you ocoul Not keep a Set of book.but what you had Learned would do you a lot of Good it would at least Give Some knowledge of Book keepin When you sawit, and Dr and A Cr did you Experiance in the Store Give you the Right for a Peromtion, I dont think So How about the Ford Place I don think so Well I thought being you and Sandro were Going to get at Least Seventy five Percent of what I had work for and Still am All of My Live that you would come And Not Take ove the Ranch but Carry out My Instructions Until We at least got it out of Det but you dot want to do that Alot of my Mistakes is been Caused from Listing to others One was when Dr McQuenn kept after Me Until I spent Forty Eight Thousand Dollars on Jack Hindmand and Hard hi m as a Cow Forman that is why he Left because he wanted to run the Ranch and I would Not let him this is the same reason I am Not going to Turn the Ranch over to you If I did not Care any thing for you Sandra and the Kid I would do it Some Smart Elex would be waiting to Tare you To Pieces John Hathaway for one all this mess Come up here Christmas Was All uncall for just by some one Meddlin in where they hav no businessMoving away from Murdock was one of the Big est Fool things I everheard of as for the Room on the House it would been built to long ago I told you I would get it and I allways do what I say, if you had wanted Me to let you Run the Ranch would have been to have Carried out My orders,which you did not do when I would ask you why you hadent done these things I would ask you Later what would you Tell Me you would Say I dont Know Howe would you l ike to have Some one that you had working for you and you would ask him some times

After 5 days, return to
MURDOCK MERCANTILE CO.,
MURDOCK, FLA.

PUNTA GORDA JUN 12 7 PM 1954 FLA.

UNITED STATES POSTAGE 3 CENTS

Via Air Mail

Mr. A. P. Frizzell
Rt. 1.
Clarks Lake, Michigan
% C. J. Claire

> I hope I have made a good deal, but with no one to help me run it, there was not much else left for me to do. Of course, I will have four years yet, so if you want to come back and think you can work with me, that will be all right. I don't think you would have trouble working for me, if you would just carry out instructions.
>
> I work a lot of other people, and they don't seem to have any trouble. If they did, they would leave, and they are not going to get any of it in my will, so you can make up your mind to do whatever you want to. That is entirely up to you.
>
> Hope all of you are well and having good time.
> Dad 6/24/54 Murdock, Fla

Granddaddy had sold 78,000 acres to "Mall," as he called it. His deal was the largest land deal between private parties in the history of the state of Florida at the time, and it appeared in the headlines of every major Florida newspaper.

The deal was really a sale to Chemical Research Corporation, which owned control of Maule Industries of Miami, an affiliate of West Coast Development Company. Maule was the south's largest concrete products manufacturing firm. Alto Orr, Uncle Tilley's brother-in-law, was a real estate broker by then, and he handled the deal.

Excluding the El Jobean tract, the property stretched from the Myakka River to the Peace River and fronted on Charlotte Harbor for a total of more than twenty-five miles of waterfront. Highway 41 traversed the property for just under thirty miles, and the railroad ran through it for about fifteen miles. The tract included the 35,000 acres in Sarasota County that Granddaddy had bought from Ringling Brothers in the 1940s.

He sold the entire tract for $2,300,000, of which $248,900 was for the Sarasota County Ringling property. Granddaddy's attorney Leo Wotitzky, one of several prominent Punta Gorda attorneys, told me that when Granddaddy went to Miami to close the deal, he asked for the down payment with three separate checks in the amount of $100,000 each, because he did not want any one person to know all of his business.

Dear Paul Sandra and all other 4
Got Your Card thanks. Well You Said
You were Going to the Dr to see if he Could
Put his finger on what is the mater with
You. Well that you Can do more Than any
One Else You seef if You Make up Your mine To
do so they is nothing the matter with You That You
Cant Streighten out Your seef and untill you
make up Your mine to to do it You Seef You
Will be just like this, to begin with if You
Had told me that if You Could Just Go some
where here in Florida to be quiet and Rest for
10 Days I would have believed You meant it
and I Cared becase it would do You some Good
but when You Wanted to Light out on about
4000 Mill Trip and on Road All time I Could
not see it. I Expect to take a vacation for 10
Day about Aug 1st but it will be on the beach
Some where Here where I Can be rested when
I Get back and Can be Got by phone when They
want me. We are Still Going with all Machines
I think I Can finish in 2 Weeks then I am bring
Everything in clean it up and paint it some repair
then I am Going to see if Can Get some Jobs for it
And the men with some Road Contractor if Cant
I will Lay them off. Well Paul I have sold the Ranch
to more it will take 90 Day to Close Deal I am to have
4 Years to use it before I turn it over to them any

About three months later on September 21, Granddaddy made a mortgage deed with Florida West Coast Land Development Company for $950,000 in Charlotte County and $868,867.06 in Sarasota County, a portion of which was for the Ringling property. The mortgage was payable with eighteen promissory notes in the amount of $101,048.17 each at 2.5 percent, the first one on or before two years, and the rest annually, not to "succeed" seventeen years and could be prepaid without penalty.

After the sale, Granddaddy expressed doubt about it to different ones in the family. He said perhaps he should have sold only the area south of the Tamiami Trail and kept the area north of it to continue the cattle business.

In the end, he reassured himself and others, "It would take me too long to develop it and do it like it should be done."[5]

It was hard for him to think of ending his cattle business. He was proud of his cattle, and he said, "I have one of the outstanding Brahman herds to be found anywhere in the state."[6]

The deal did include grazing rights for his cattle on a portion of the land that would remain with him for ten years, which was the length of time he was given to round up all of the cattle. It also included timber rights.

After the sale was final, Granddaddy sat on the front porch of Aunt Nellie's house, and he told her, "One day there will be a house for every cow." Aunt Nellie repeated his vision to me on that same front porch thirty years later, in about 1985, and I figured it was true right about then.

Two years after Granddaddy made the sale, on October 24, 1956, the Mackle Brothers announced plans to build 1,000 homes on 5,000 acres of the Charlotte County land that was once Granddaddy's ranch. They said that they had already built 100 homes.

At the time, it was described as the beginning of the biggest housing development in the world. Granddaddy *was* a man with vision.

In the fall of 1954, Granddaddy added Frizzell Realty to his ever-growing list of enterprises. He started listing and advertising property for sale.

> October 24, 1954
> THREE FURNISHED APARTMENT HOUSES FOR SALE - One has 3 apartments, $12,500, down payment $500, terms $75 per month. Another has 6 apartments,

> 2 cottages, $23,500, down payment $10,000, terms. Royal Palms. Gross income last season $3000. Punta Gorda residential section. One has 8 apartments, price $25,000. Downtown Ft. Myers. Write Frizzell Realty, Murdock, Florida.

Mother would later become a real estate broker and use the same name, Frizzell Realty, to do business in El Jobean, where she would develop the El Jobean tract that had all become hers. She would build streets and canals and sell lots there. She was another amazing success story, but that's another book.

> November 13, 1954
> FOR SALE: Brand new never been used 1 D8 Caterpillar Tractor. Bulldozer and stumper. Carries new machine guarantee by manufacturer. Will sell for $2,000 less than list price. Will deliver up to 150 miles. A. C. Frizzell, Murdock, Fla.

Christmas rolled around that year, and Granddaddy did what he had done for many years and made sure that Santa stopped at Murdock. Santa arrived at the Mercantile in the back of a World War II Jeep with a bag full of gifts marked "boy" and another bag marked "girl" for all of the Murdock children, including my siblings and myself.

Forty years before on December 20, 1914, one of Murdock's first young settlers had written a letter to *The Tampa Tribune* expressing anxiety about Santa finding her there.

> December 20, 1914
> APPEALS OF SMALL FOLKS FOR CHRISTMAS CHEER:
> "I am a little girl eight years old, and I never have been to school but my sister teaches me at home and I am in the second grade. We live so far in the country I was afraid Santa Claus would not come to see me this year if I didn't write to him. I want you to bring me a big doll, a doll bed and a yard of ribbon for my hair. Murdock."

"Waiting for Santa in Murdock"
(Cherry, A. C., and Steve in the front).

Back at home on Christmas Eve, Granddaddy gave each of us five new, crisp, one-dollar bills, which is what he gave us every year.

Not much happened in the year 1955 after the sale of the ranch.

In the spring, the McQueens took a group of Methodist juniors for a hayride through Frizzell pastures. They picked wildflowers and roasted weiners. Doc McQueen was the county agent at the time.

> March 5, 1955
> FOR SALE
> 300 WHITE Wyandotte and 500 New Hampshire Red
> young laying chickens, laying just four months.
> A. C. Frizzell
> Murdock, Florida

In August, we were back in Michigan at Grandpa Claire's cabin on a lake up there. Jack Hindman was there, too.

Jack Hindman and Daddy at Grandpa's cabin in Michigan, August 1955.

In September, Uncle Forney was back working in the Mercantile, and in October, Granddaddy donated a car from his Ford Place to Charlotte High School to be used for driver training courses.

Then on November 30, thieves again broke into the Mercantile. They may have been two convicts who had escaped from a road gang. They stole $3000 in cash and a few checks. They broke the lock on the door and chiseled off the combination dials of two safes. In one of the safes, they overlooked a ring valued at $1,000. They also stole fifteen cartons of cigarettes, candy, some loaves of bread, $75 worth of lunch meat, shot gun shells, size 38 men's clothes, women's dungarees, and children's clothes.[7]

And that was it for 1955.

1956, on the other hand, was a very different story. It began with Daddy starting his own business, and everything that followed led to a raging forest fire in the end. It was a very explosive year.

In January, Daddy finalized a deal that he had begun in October to buy one new Northwest Model 25 dragline from Florida-Georgia Tractor Company for $26,012.15, payable $3,000 down and $1,150.75 per month for nineteen months with no interest. Then, he went to work.

At his first job, a seawall construction project at Punta Gorda Beach, his 45-year-old foreman, Morris Davis, received second and third degree burns when a pump he was filling exploded. A black man working nearby saw him, covered in flames, jump into the water. The man hurried over and pushed him under water to extinguish the fire.

Then in March, the Charlotte County Commissioners awarded Daddy his second job. It was a half of a contract to do some ditching, having made an identical bid with another person.

While Daddy was busy working on his Punta Gorda projects, a murder took place on the ranch.

Willie Wells, one of Granddaddy's cowboys, lived at a camp on Granddaddy's ranch in the Hammock Ponds area. Willie was age 55, and his wife was age 15 and a seventh grade student.

They had been separated for about six months, when Willie suddenly jumped from the bushes where his young wife was staying. He aimed a 16-gauge shotgun at her and at the couple with whom she lived, and he threatened them. The couple ran inside the house.

Then, he told his wife that she had to talk to him, or he would kill her. She replied that she would rather be dead.

Apparently, he believed her, and he shot her dead. Willie claimed she had a grip on the shotgun at the time.

He voluntarily surrendered at the Courthouse.[8]

Two years before, there had been another murder on the ranch. In June 1954, at the same time that Granddaddy was selling the ranch, he had leased three section houses in Murdock from Seaboard Air Line Railroad Company for an annual rental of $60 to be used for residential purposes. He would pay utilities and taxes. He probably leased them for more homes for his workers, maybe even for the ill-fated worker named Levens.

A week later, Levens went on a wildcat hunt with his ten-year-old stepson and two other men, one named Hooker. Around 2:00am, their truck stalled about three miles from Murdock.

The men, who had been drinking, slept until 7:00am, when they sent Levens' stepson to a Frizzell camp for help. While he was gone, Levens fought with Hooker, and Hooker killed Levens when he broke his neck with the butt of a .22 rifle. Their argument had started over who would go for help.[9]

A month after the Willie Wells incident, Granddaddy shocked the whole county. On the evening of April 21, 1956, at the age of 66, he married his longtime much younger girlfriend, Dorothy Carey, age 37, at the Murdock home of Mr. and Mrs. Bailey, his bookkeeper and wife, in a simple ceremony in a room filled with gladioli and white mums. Rev. Joe A. Rainey, pastor of the El Jobean Baptist Church performed the single-ring ceremony.

"Mrs. Frizzell wore a blue gown with white accessories, and Mrs. Bailey a pink one with white accessories. Both wore orchid corsages." There were six other guests.[10]

Before settling at Murdock, Granddaddy and Dorothy went to Nassau for a two-week honeymoon, but they only stayed for a couple of days. They returned from Nassau to Miami on a Pan American World Airways flight on April 25th.

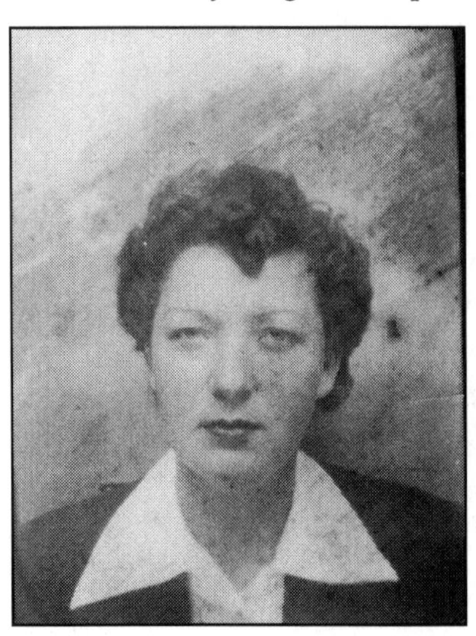

Family lore has it that Granddaddy met Dorothy when she worked as a barmaid at his favorite hangout for thirty years, the notorious roadhouse, then known as Alligator Bar, but previously The Acline Wine Place. She was originally from Georgia transplanted to Tampa and had served in the Women's Army Corps for about the last six months of World War II. Then in 1946, she was one of five women veterans who took flight training in Tampa. By 1950, when she wrecked Granddaddy's car, she was a nurse in Punta Gorda, and in 1951, she was living in Murdock, where she would stay. Her nephew said that she was Granddaddy's secretary there.

When Granddaddy proposed to Dorothy, he first asked her if she could cook. When she replied yes, then he asked her to marry him.

In June, we again went to Grandpa Claire's cabin in Michigan and back to Florida in July, when Daddy, who had added hauling to his work list, used his trucks for hauling sand for the new Punta Gorda Beach.

Daddy's next job was digging canals at Harbor Heights, and by then he had a girlfriend Kitty whose parents lived there. Kitty was married and lived in Louisiana, but she visited her parents in Harbor Heights.

> September 15, 1956, Ft. Myers News Press
> MAN for general store, meat, groceries, dry goods,

sundries, gasoline and oil.
Apply A. C. Frizzell, Murdock, Fla.

September 15, 1956
DAIRY - Known as Sunshine Dairy near Palmetto, Fla. 400 acres good land all cleared and planted in tame grasses. Fine dairy barn all equipped, 4 tenant houses. Good milk base. 200 dairy cows. Price complete $185,000 or will sell without cattle. For full particulars contact A. C. Frizzell, Murdock, Fla.

On November 5, 1956, Charlotte County residents voted to set up forest fire control for the protection of rural homes and wooded land. Charlotte County was the only west coast county in Florida without fire control. "The county's timber potential is rated by the state service as probably the best of any county in southwest Florida."[11]

Four fire towers would be built, one of them in El Jobean and named for Granddaddy. He donated an acre of land for it.

Frizzell Forestry Tower, El Jobean, 2010.

There is a street in El Jobean named Frizzell, too, and four canals named Cheryl, Steven, Alan, and Merry, but nobody knows who they are. It is very strange to me. Granddaddy's name used to be a household word in southwest Florida all the way from Tampa to Miami. Everybody knew who he was. Everybody had at least one story to tell about him. He was a living legend. Now, nobody knows his name.

Ironically, a couple of weeks after the fire control vote, "one of Florida's wealthiest cattlemen" and three of his workers were arrested for careless pasture burning and charged with permitting the fire to spread. Granddaddy had ordered his workers to set fire to some of his own pastureland that he wanted cleared, but the fire burned out of control and severely burned the pine timber on over 5,300 acres of land near Englewood in Sarasota County. Fortunately, no people were harmed and no houses were damaged. They would all go to trial in Sarasota County.[12]

On February 2, 1957, Daddy bought cattle from Granddaddy and gave him a mortgage in the amount of $25,300 for the following:

> All of the Brahman type cattle, being all of the cattle owned by the Mortgagor constituting approximately 900 head located in the Counties of Charlotte and Sarasota, and on the lands heretofore owned by A. C. Frizzell, and bearing the following marks and brands, to-wit;
>
> One portion of said cattle being marked – Crop split one ear, Crop under Bit in other; and branded "P"

> Another portion of said cattle being marked – Crop in one ear, Swallow Fork under Bit in other, and being also branded "P"
>
> The remainder of said cattle being branded AP

Daddy was still running his own business, but he was planning to do some ranching, too, on his Kings Highway property.

Later in February, the Seaboard Railroad started shipping watermelons from Arcadia. The watermelons had been grown on about 1,000 acres that the area's leading ranchers had allowed growers from Florida and Georgia to use. 400 of those acres were Granddaddy's near Murdock, and three different growers had used them. The Vanderbilt Two-V Ranch grew about 450 acres, 150 of which one of the Vanderbilt brothers grew himself.[13]

Then in May, one of Daddy's black workers ran into a school bus with one of Daddy's dump trucks. The bus had stopped to unload some children, when the truck rear-ended it. Nobody was hurt, but damage was estimated at $300. Insurance covered it. The worker was charged with reckless driving and failure to control his vehicle. He was thrown into the county jail.[14]

A month later in June, Granddaddy bought Rigell Lumber and Supply Company, his second lumber yard in Punta Gorda. At the same time, his brother Roy bought the Lincoln-Mercury dealership in Ft. Myers and named it Frizzell Lincoln-Mercury. For the last thirty-five years, Roy had worked in the lumber, tractor, hardware, and real estate businesses.[15]

Other than the lumber yard purchase, during the second half of the 1950s, Granddaddy's real estate transactions were not what they once had been, but they were quite enough to keep him busy. He bought and sold lots and buildings in Punta Gorda, El Jobean, and Fort Myers; he built houses; he carried first and second mortgages; he even carried chattel mortgages, such as one for a Ford Sedan and a Mobile Home House Trailer.

On June 29, his lifelong friend and neighbor Daniel Child died at the age of 81. Daniel's diaries are his legacy, and much more of a legacy than he would have ever imagined. Besides a few articles in the archives of a few newspapers, Daniel Child's diaries alone tell the story of early Murdock, and they tell it in great detail. The diaries are a virtually unknown treasure that the Charlotte County Historical Society has preserved. They were of great value to me in writing this book.

About a month later on August 6, Granddaddy's brother Forney had a heart attack and died at his home in Sycamore, Georgia. All of his Frizzell relatives attended his funeral, including Granddaddy, Daddy and Mother. Uncle Forney's wife Ann Freeman would die sixteen years later in Sycamore, after spending two years in a nursing home.

The next year in March 1958, construction began on our new home to be located at 625 W. Olympia Avenue in Punta Gorda. A couple of blocks west of our current home, it was built on two or three city lots. Built in an L-shape on two sides of a 20' by 40' swimming pool, it had a master bedroom and two large bedrooms divided by partitions, making a total of five bedrooms with three bathrooms and the most modern conveniences at the time.

On April 3, 1958, Daddy won a bid for about 4,000 yards of fill dirt for Baker Academy in Punta Gorda. Baker Academy was to be a new elementary school, grades one through eight, for black children.[16]

A couple of weeks later, Daddy donated his equipment and fill for a diamond for Punta Gorda's Little League, to which belonged about sixty boys, including my two brothers. I remember I wanted to play, too, but girls were not allowed.

One year after Uncle Forney died, on August 29, 1958, Uncle Roy had a heart attack and died at age 51 in Ft. Myers. Services were held at the Charlotte Harbor Cemetery, where he was buried in the Frizzell family plot with his mother and father.[17]

After only a couple of years, Daddy went out of business, and so on October 10, 1958, Granddaddy and Dorothy gave Mother and Daddy a Warranty Deed for the entire El Jobean tract, which ran about four and a half miles along the Myakka River and totaled about 4,000 acres. Same date, Granddaddy gave them a Mortgage Deed in the amount of $50,000, payable $5,000 per year at 2.5% interest.

Daddy and Mother then set up a single-wide trailer with a porch for an office at El Jobean, and they started developing land. They put in a couple of streets, and they built a couple of canals. But Daddy's drinking was getting worse, and Mother was soon on her own.

Charlotte County was booming, though, and that would help. As of November 16, 1958, the number of building permits issued for ten months in Charlotte County had almost doubled the total for the whole year of 1957. Granddaddy was the leader for the largest new residential permit in the amount of $18,000.[18]

By February 18, 1959, Port Charlotte had 1,500 homes and about 3,000 residents and the beginnings of a city on its main street with "filling stations, hardware stores, dress shops, appliance stores and beauty shops." The Mackle Brothers were selling homesites for $895, payable $10 down and $10 per month. People from every state and Canada had bought there. At the time, the Mackle Brothers predicted that Port Charlotte would be Florida's fourth largest city behind Miami, Jacksonville, and Tampa.[19]

It is now Florida's 19th largest. Who could predict Disney World?

In late May, while our new home was still under construction, we were swimming in the pool there, when a neighbor lady attempted to drown my sister, Merry. The woman was walking by, when she saw Merry playing in the pool with a life jacket on. Without saying a word, the woman ran into the yard, jumped into the pool, and pushed Merry's head under water. I jumped in and pushed her away from Merry. Daddy then took over, called the police, and the woman was arrested and thrown in jail. She was the wife of a local attorney.[20]

Charges were dropped after the woman agreed to be treated in a hospital. She never returned to Punta Gorda.

Then on June 12, Mother and Daddy sold their first lot in El Jobean, and they sold their second lot on November 18. For every sale that they made, Granddaddy had to legally release the land to them.

On July 29, Granddaddy made an agreement with West Coast Land Company to cancel all timber and grazing rights and would vacate by September 21, five years after the sale instead of ten.

Then on August 14, I remember listening to the news on a radio at a summer camp north of Tampa. Punta Gorda's grand ol' hotel had burned to the ground with flames that could be seen for twenty-five miles around. It took firefighters from three counties five hours to get it under control. The cause of the fire was unknown, but arson was always suspected for insurance purposes.

The hotel, one of the first buildings in the area, had been a hub for Punta Gorda social and recreational life since it opened in 1888 at the end of the railroad. It had attracted many outstanding and wealthy visitors, it had hosted social events for the locals, and it had served as a playground for Punta Gorda children. Our parents had attended new year's balls there with extravagant banquets and intricate ice sculptures, and we children had played in the empty Olympic-size pool and in the abandoned gardens there; we had played on the seawall, throwing rocks at stingrays in the bay; we had climbed in the giant banyon tree nearby. The hotel was so much more than a landmark; it was the skyline of Punta Gorda.

The hotel was gone now, and Murdock was disappearing. As a part of his land deal, Granddaddy had agreed to move all of his Murdock buildings about a mile south on Highway 41, where Cochran Boulevard is today. Besides a church and the Mercantile, there were about twenty homes that he moved, all because his workers wanted to stay with him. The homes were later torn down to extend Cochran Boulevard, and the General Store later became Desoto Groves with a post office located where the "Whites Only" bathroom used to be.

U.S. Post Office next to Desoto Groves in Murdock. Not before 1969. Color slide. State Archives of Florida, Florida Memory. <https://www.floridamemory.com/items/show/317600>, (accessed 26 March 2018)

Four days after the hotel fire, with the Murdock buildings gone, the Charlotte County Commissioners voted to change the name from Murdock to Port Charlotte. By then, the only building left there was the home of the man once known as "Mr. Murdock."

A "Murdock" highway sign still stood, and it stood very much alone, identifying the place where an old southern town had once been the headquarters for one man's empire. It is now listed as one of Charlotte County's "Lost Towns."

Change was blowin' in the wind, and it was blowin' fast.

In that same month, we finally moved into our new home at 625 W. Olympia and left behind our little house where we had lived for our first five and a half years in Punta Gorda.

We would leave our childhoods there, at 508 W. Olympia, and life would never be the same. Not ever.

A couple of months after we moved into our new home, in October, Granddaddy and Dorothy moved into their new home that he had built for her on forty acres he had reserved for himself on Highway 41 south of where he moved the Murdock houses. His nephew Uncle Roy's son, William, was the architect, and they had started construction of the house in February. Called Murdock Acres, it would be a Charlotte County landmark for about thirty years.

The big, fancy, ranch-style brick house with a blue front door was a most impressive site to behold from Highway 41. A long, paved driveway wound through moss-covered, stately oak trees from the highway to the house, where it circled and branched off to a garage and around the whole house. Six hundred and fifty red-flowering ixoras lined the driveway on both sides and two life-size stone horse statues flanked the front gate.

I remember the inside of the house. Thick, white carpet covered its floors, and Dorothy made us take off our shoes at the front door. The foyer opened to a great room that reached to the sky and was separated from an all-white kitchen on the right by a breakfast bar. The great room stretched to a lanai on the back of the house that was furnished with white wrought iron tables and chairs with blue cushions. The furniture was over-sized to fit Granddaddy.

In the front of the house, Granddaddy's office was on the right with cypress paneling and a western motif, and the bedrooms were on the left. The master bedroom was pink with two full-size beds in it. All of the furniture in the house was pecan wood, and there was an intercom system that connected every room.

Thirty years later in the 1980s, I was living in Charlotte County, and I remember passing by the house and watching it being demolished, brick by brick. I remember the day the house was gone, and the two horse statues disappeared. Nothing was left. Nothing.

Next time I looked, a Days Inn stood there.

For our first Christmas in our new home, Daddy gave us all fur gifts. He gave Mother a mink stole, my sister and me rabbit capes, and my brothers coonskin hats. Mother took her mink stole on our next summer trip up north, and she wore it with her peddle pushers and loafers when we went into a restaurant for lunch. She said she could not leave it in the car, because it needed to breathe.

On December 30th, Daddy and Mother sold our previous home at 508 West Olympia. They sold it for $11,500, payable $80 down and $80 per month at 6.5 percent interest.

Within days, Daddy then voluntarily committed himself for alcoholism treatment to Anclote Manor, a private mental hospital in Tarpon Springs, where he underwent individual and group psychotherapy.

Anclote Manor

The place was located on twenty-two acres that fronted on the Anclote River. It was originally built in 1928 and called Sunset Hills Country Club. Rich and famous guests from all over the country stayed there, including Al Capone. After World War II, it became a resort hotel, and in 1953, a psychiatric hospital, at which time, many renovations and additions made it a glorious sanitarium for the wealthy. Each patient had his or her own individual psychiatrist, psychologist, medical doctor, nurse, and social worker. Many pioneers in the mental health field worked there.[21]

Quite some time after Daddy's stay there, the 130-bed facility changed names several times, went downhill, and gained a terrible reputation, even being called "a medieval house of horrors." It eventually closed in 1997, and the building was demolished in 2006.

The property now holds a large gated community with expensive townhomes.

But when Daddy stayed there, it was still a glorious place, and it was too much of a fun resort for him and his wealthy buddies to benefit much from their time there. For example, they were allowed nights out on the town to go to the movies or whatever they wanted to do, and Daddy was spending a lot of money keeping up with his new friends, among them Ross Allen and Rick Hammel.

Ross Allen was a world-famous snake hunter at the time. He established the Reptile Institute, which was a tourist attraction at Silver Springs for forty-six years, and he was president of the International Crocodile Society, but most important, he developed many anti-venoms resulting from his work with poisonous snakes.

I remember when I was at summer camp, Ross Allen's wife Virginia came to give us children a talk about snakes. She displayed one in a glass box. We watched it swallow a frog whole and saw the frog's shape slide down the length of the snake's thin, round body.

Ross tried to talk Daddy into going on a snake collecting expedition with him to South America. Daddy, who did not share Ross's zeal for snakes, declined the invitation.

Daddy's other buddy at Anclote Manor was Rick Hammel, the president of Pillsbury at the time. Rick was a multi-millionaire from St. Louis. His wealth came from flour mills and cake mixes. He built a home in Naples, Florida, and Daddy would spend a lot of time there, driving his boat while the two of them fished. He also spent a lot of time with Rick in St. Louis. They stayed best buddies until Rick died.

About two months into Daddy's five-month stay at Anclote Manor, on March 5, 1960, Granddaddy wrote a letter to Mother. I have paraphrased and paragraphed it for ease of reading.

> Sandra 3/5/60
>
> I am sending you a check for here for $125.00 per week. As you know, Paul is not there now and has not been for 2 month, which you should not owe any bills.

> [Daddy had been running up big bills at the bars all over town.]
>
> Now also, I have paid several hundred dollars from out here, since Paul has been up there, besides Paul's bills up there have been over a thousand dollars per month, and the last of this month will be 3 months.
>
> By that time, if he is not better, I cannot promise to keep on doing what I am for you all, as I am not physically able to work and feeling as well, and too, what I had done and have done is not appreciated.
>
> I told Paul when he got out that I wanted him to forget about me or to work in any place I had or might fix, that you and he to work out your own way and leave me out of it, as you have already told me that Paul was doing alright, until I told the bank not to loan him anymore money, and now I will not interfere.
>
> I hope you and Paul work out things to you and his satisfaction, and it will be much better in the future than it has in the past.
>
> A. C.

While Daddy was still in Anclote Manor, on the 30th of March, Granddaddy's sister Vona died at age 65 in Ft. Myers. She was buried in the Frizzell family plot in Charlotte Harbor with her brother, Roy, and their parents. In the last three years, Granddaddy had buried three of his siblings, his oldest brother Lon Forney, his youngest brother Roy, and his sister Vona. The remaining three would outlive him.

About a week later on April 6, somebody left a three-day old baby girl on the seat of a winter visitor's car during Presbyterian church services in Punta Gorda. The car was parked nearby under the banyon tree at the bayfront. Dorothy decided she wanted to adopt the baby girl, and Granddaddy agreed, if she would be named for

Granny, "Miss Pattie," and so they named the baby Patti Lee, and they adopted her. The adoption was finalized on October 30. Granddaddy was 70 years old, and Dorothy was 41.

Sandra 3/5/60

I Am Sending You a Ck
for here for $125.00 Per week As
You know. Paul is not there now
And has not been for 2 Months Which
You Should not owe Any bills Now
Also I have Paid Several hundred Dollars
from out here Since Paul has been
~~And You know~~ up there besides Pauls bills
up there has been up there over a Thousand
Dollars Per Month And the Last of this
Month Will be 3 Months. by that time if
he is not better I Can not Prompest to
Keep on Doweing What I Am for You
All. As I Am not Fusicaly able to work
And Finacy So Well And to What I had
done And I have done is not apreated
I told Paul when he Gotten out that
I Wanted him to for Get abut me
or to work in Any Place I had or
might Fix that You And he to Work
out You Own way. And leave Me out
it. As You have Already told me
that Paul Was doing Alright untile I
told the Bank not to loane him
Any more money. And Now I Will not
interfair I Hope You And Paul Work
out things to Your And his Satisfaction
And it Will be Much better in the Futher
than it has in the Past

A.C

A couple of months later, Granddaddy wrote to Daddy, still at Anclote Manor:

> May 10, 1960
> Dear Paul,
> You will recall I told you you could use the car this week as you want to plan on leaving the car at the Garage when you come down this week.
>
> I am going to have to tell them there at Anclote Manor that I cannot pay these cash amounts you are drawing there each week. On April 4 it was $49.56, April 11, $45.05, April 18, $22.90, and April 25, $61.59, a total for four weeks of $179.14. Something in reason is all right such as $10.00 or $12.00 a week.
>
> You must remember that you are not up there to have a big time. You have told me you are there to get yourself straightened out so that you can soon assume the responsibilities of taking care of your family. You must realize that you have the responsibility and obligation to fulfill.
>
> The Anclote Manor bill for the past four weeks was $1,115.64 including the cash you received as outlined above, The Blue Cross made a payment of $250.00. Check for the balance of $865.54 is enclosed.
>
> I hope you will realize you have to stand on your own 2 feet. No one else can do this for you.
>
> ACF:B

Daddy checked out of Anclote Manor at the end of that month of May, but he would return around November 1st.

May 10, 1960

Mr. A. P. Frizzell
Anclote Manor
P. O. Drawer 8
Tarpon Springs, Florida

Dear Paul:

You will recall I told you you could use the car this week so you want to plan on leaving the car at the Garage when you come down this week.

I am going to have to tell them there at Anclote Manor that I can not pay these cash amounts you are drawing there each week. On April 4 it was $49.58 - April 11, $45.05 - April 18, $22.90 and April 25, $61.59 a total for four weeks of $179.14. Something in reason is all right such as $10.00 or $12.00 a week.

You must remember that you are not up there to have a big time. You have told me you are there to get yourself straightened out so that you can soon assume the responsibilities of taking care of your family. You must realize that you have the responsibility and obligation to fulfill.

The Anclote Manor bill for the past four weeks was $1,115.64 including the cash you received as outlined above. The Blue Cross made a payment of $250.00. Check for the balance of $865.34 is enclosed.

I hope you will realize you have to stand on your own 2 feet. No one else can do this for you.

ACF:D

On June 15, Granddaddy's Frizzell Lumber Company had a four-day grand opening for brand new buildings that covered an entire block in Ft. Myers. They totaled 32,000 square feet and cost $250,000. Uncle Roy's son William, by then well known as an outstanding architect in the area, was the designer.

The business was very similar to a modern-day Home Depot. It had twenty-two departments, in addition to a tool rental, a customer planning center, and a paint center that boasted the latest in paint-mixing machines.

During the four-day opening, merchandise was marked down, and the first 150 women each day received a free potted plant. There was a free door prize on the last day of the event.[22]

Granddaddy's Ft. Myers lumberyard had grown into a giant Mercantile, a precursor of Home Depot!

Only three months after its opening, on September 10, Hurricane Donna hit the southwest coast of Florida with eleven-foot surges and

130-mile-per-hour wind gusts. It was so strong that it blew all the water out of the Caloosahatchee and Peace Rivers into the Gulf of Mexico. It drained the Peace River so much that you could walk across from Charlotte Harbor to Punta Gorda. Then when the eye passed north, it brought the water back in, causing the heaviest damage. Donna was one of the all-time great hurricanes. It left behind 364 direct fatalities.

In Ft. Myers, it completely blew the roof off Granddaddy's new lumberyard building; in Punta Gorda, it damaged over 1,000 homes. It blew off the roofs of almost every home in a new upscale subdivision called Punta Gorda Isles, about one mile west of our new home, but it did not damage our home. Daddy had built it to withstand hurricanes, and we stayed there the whole time. He boarded up the glass doors around the swimming pool and most of the windows, we filled the three bathtubs with water, and we sat tight. I remember looking through the kitchen window and watching bicycles, trees, lawn furniture, and all kinds of things blow by. An oak tree in our yard stood firm, even though it bounced up and down, and its roots heaved the ground up and down, trying to take flight. That ol' oak tree was still standing in 2010.

After the storm, the newspaper started a Hurricane Donna Club and gave everybody who had survived it a card entitling them to talk about their Donna experience as much as they wanted.

From then on, September 10 was called Donna Destruction Day.

Around November 1st, Daddy returned to Anclote Manor, and a few weeks later, we moved to Tarpon Springs to be near him. We lived in a small two-bedroom rented house. The four of us children piled into one bedroom that was wall-to-wall beds, and we all attended school in Tarpon Springs for about three weeks before the Christmas break.

> December 12, 1960
> BOOKKEEPER experienced in Retail Lumber preferably in the age group between 35 and 50, Address A. C. Frizzell, P. O. Box 7, Murdock, Fla.

On December 19, two of Granddaddy's houses where his workers lived in Murdock burned to the ground. One of the houses was where Hattie and Sammie King lived. Fire department volunteers kept the fire from spreading to other nearby houses. The fire was caused by an overheated stove, and loss to Granddaddy was estimated at $7,000.[23]

Eleven days later on December 30, Granddaddy made an agreement for deed with Hattie and Sammie for a house in Punta Gorda for $10,500, payable for only one dollar down and $80 per month.

A week after Granddaddy provided the Kings with a new home, on Friday morning, January 6, 1961, Daddy came charging into our little Tarpon Springs house and yelled at Mother to come out of the bathroom. She was taking a shower, and she did not come out.

Daddy banged on the closed bathroom door with his fists, and he hollered with great emotion and distress, tears running down his face, "DADDY'S DEAD! DADDY'S DEAD!"

Granddaddy, then age 70, had died suddenly of a heart attack at his home early that morning. We rushed back to Punta Gorda.

The whole county mourned. There were hundreds of people, both black and white, from near and far, at Granddaddy's funeral service at two o'clock Sunday afternoon in the little Charlotte Harbor Baptist Church that he had attended for decades. Inside the church, people sat crammed into the pews and stood packed into the aisles. Outside in the shade of huge oak trees, people stood crowded in the yard, many on tiptoe, stretching to see through the open windows and the open front doors of the little wooden church.

Granddaddy was, of course, buried in the Frizzell family plot at the Charlotte Harbor Cemetery with his brother Roy, his sister Vona, and their parents. A Masonic graveside service was held there, where the display of flowers decorating his grave was said to be the largest in the history of Charlotte County.

News of the death of "Charlotte County's most noted citizen" appeared in every major newspaper in Florida: Pensacola, Tallahassee, Ft. Lauderdale, Miami, as well as Tampa, Sarasota, Ft. Myers, and many others. They all told the story of the millionaire cattle rancher land baron, who had started as a railroad clerk and built himself an empire in the wilds of Southwest Florida.

A close business associate said it all, "With the death of Mr. Frizzell, an important era in the history of this part of Florida has come to an end. His passing will be severely felt for a long time by many people with whom he had close personal, family, and business ties."

EPILOGUE

For six years after Granddaddy's death, the family fought in Court over his will. It was the largest probate in the history of Charlotte County at the time, but by the time it was all over, the attorneys got more than anybody else ... almost.

The estate was finally settled on February 1, 1967. After debts, expenses, and Daddy's share were paid, Dorothy received her one-third dower's interest, and Patti Lee received her one-third. Another third of the estate was divided equally among Granddaddy's siblings or their heirs and Granny's two children, a total of ten heirs.

Daddy was treated separately with cash and a trust fund, payable to his four children upon his death. Daddy also received the El Jobean property after Granddaddy's bank forgave the $50,000 mortgage on it. It also forgave the $25,000 mortgage on the cattle Daddy had bought from Granddaddy. Daddy had sold the cattle for $78,000, but only collected $20,000. The buyer had written him a bad check for the balance, and Daddy was unable to collect. Separately, Granddaddy also left the four of us trust funds for our educations.

Five attorneys split an amount equal to one-third.

Almost two years after Granddaddy's death, in the fall of 1962, Daddy and Mother divorced, and Daddy married his longtime girlfriend Kitty eleven days later. They left Charlotte County and eventually lived on Pine Island.

As a part of their divorce settlement, Daddy had signed over the El Jobean property to Mother, and she spent most of the rest of her life living and working in a mobile home there. She had received no money from Granddaddy or Daddy, and she struggled to make it, but she did. All by herself, she developed the land, put in roads and canals, sold the lots on time, and managed to pay land taxes in the amount of $20,000 per year. Eventually, she sold large chunks of the vast property and then finally sold it all. She bought a nice home in Jacksonville and moved there.

Daddy and Mother are both deceased. Daddy had a heart attack and died at home in 1988 at the age of 64. Mother died in 1992 of complications from emphysema at the age of 65.

As for the four of us, Merry died in 2006 at the young age of 53; my brothers and I currently live in North Florida. A. C. and his wife Natalie live near me in the Panhandle on the Gulf coast south of Tallahassee; Steve and his wife Brenda live on the St. John's River south of Jacksonville. All four of us each has one child of the opposite sex. Steve is the CEO for a computer software company; A. C. is a retired college professor. As for me, that's another book.

ENDNOTES

The Promised Land

1. Milton Plumb, "Million-Dollar Success Story Working Couple Builds 200,000-Acre Ranch," *The Tampa Sunday Tribune,* August 29, 1948.

2. Florida Railroad Company website; "Florida Logging Railroads," http://www.flarr.com/lumbercos.htm, accessed December 23, 2018.

3. "Woman Candidate for Clerk Circuit Court," *The Tampa Tribune,* October 15, 1920.

Turpentine and Timber

1. Vernon Peeples, *Punta Gorda and the Charlotte Harbor Area,* Norfolk/Virginia Beach: The Donning Company, 1986, 72.

2. Sam Mase, "A.C. Frizzell - Murdock Man Went From $68 to $2,300,000," *The Tampa Tribune,* July, 1954.

3. Milton Plumb, "Million-Dollar Success Story Working Couple Builds 200,000-Acre Ranch," *The Tampa Sunday Tribune,* August 29, 1948.

4. "Punta Gorda Man Severely Burned with Flaming Gas," *The Tampa Times,* September 6, 1924.

5. *Where to Stop A Guide to the Best Hotels in the World,* Published by Moses King, Boston, Massachusetts, 1894-1895.

6. Sam Mase.

7. Ibid.

8. Thanks to good friend of the family Fred Farris for his chapter on The Acline Wine Place in *Once Upon a Time in Southwest Florida,* Venice, Florida: Gondolier Publishing Company, 1982, 93-97.

9. Vernon Peeples, 126.

10. Lindsey Williams website, "CIA Held Secret Training in Webb Wildlife Area," July 31, 1994, http://www.lindseywilliams.org/index.htm?Articles/CIA_Held_Secret_Training_In_Webb_Wildlife_Area.htm~mainFrame, accessed December 23, 2018.

11. "Mother Regains Children ...", *The Tampa Tribune,* May 5, 1928.

12. Charlotte County, Florida, website; "Cape Haze Pioneer Trail Along a Circa 1907 Railway," http://www.charlottecountyfl.com/CommunityServices/CapeHazeTrailBrochure.pdf, accessed December 23, 2018.

13. Michael Bergstrom, "In 30s, Times Were Tough, Especially For Blacks." *Sarasota Herald-Tribune*. August 4, 1994, https://news.google.com/newspapers?nid=1755&dat=19940804&id=z24fAAAAIBAJ&sjid=YHwEAAAAIBAJ&pg=6672,3544174&hl=en (accessed December 31, 2018).

14. Thanks to good friend of the family Fred Farris for his chapter on The Acline Wine Place in *Once Upon a Time in Southwest Florida,* Venice, Florida: Gondolier Publishing Company, 1982, 93-97.

Cattle Ranching

1. Milton Plumb, "Million-Dollar Success Story Working Couple Builds 200,000-Acre Ranch," *The Tampa Sunday Tribune,* August 29, 1948.

2. Florida Memory Website; State Archives of Florida, *Florida Memory,* https://www.floridamemory.com/items/show/247311, accessed December 23, 2018.

3. Ibid.

4. Karen Martin, "Teacher, Students Remember School," *Sarasota Herald-Tribune,* February 16, 1989, https://news.google.com/newspapers?nid=1755&dat=19890216&id=eT8gAAAAIBAJ&sjid=XXoEAAAAIBAJ&pg=6350,478809&hl=en, accessed December 23, 2018.

5. Ibid.

6. Angie Larkin, "Old Punta Gorda," *Charlotte Sun,* May 19, 1984.

7. Ibid.

8. Wikipedia website; *Cowboy,* http://en.wikipedia.org/wiki/Cowboy, accessed December 23, 2018.

9. Lindsey Williams website; "Byron Rhode Recalls His Early Years In Punta Gorda," September 5, 1993, http://www.lindseywilliams.org/index.htm?Articles/Byron_Rhode_Recalls_His_Early_Years_In_Punta_Gorda.htm~mainFrame, accessed December 23, 2018.

10. Ibid.

11. Florida Department of Environmental Protection Website; *Cattle Dipping Vats in Florida,* https://floridadep.gov/waste/district-business-support/content/cattle-dipping-vats-cdv, accessed December 23, 2018.

12. Milton Plumb, "Million-Dollar Success Story Working Couple Builds 200,000-Acre Ranch."

13. Micheāl Bergstrom, "Black Pioneer In Charlotte County Fought For What Was His," *Sarasota Herald-Tribune,* July 8, 1993, https://news.google.com/newspapers?nid=1755&dat=19930708&id=MX8fAAAAIBAJ&sjid=vXsEAAAAIBAJ&pg=6625,2309416&hl=en, accessed December 23, 2018.

14. "Frizzells Entertain at Murdock Ranch," *Ft. Myers News Press,* October 16, 1938.

"Million-Dollar Success Story"

1. "Lumber Company Enjoined by Court," *The Tampa Times,* January 21, 1943.

2. *Orlando Sentinel,* December 14, 2011, http://www.legacy.com/obituaries/orlandosentinel/obituary.aspx?n=martha-pearle-vogt&pid=155035386, accessed May 26, 2015.

3. Custermen website, "WW2 History of the 34th 'Red Bull' Infantry Division - Training for Europe,"

http://custermen.com/ItalyWW2/Units/Division34.htm, accessed February 15, 2016.

4. An ad in the *Ft. Myers News Press,* August 19, 1949.

5. Barbara Clendinen, "Ways for Using Eggs as Main Dishes Help in Meat Shortage," *The Tampa Tribune,* April 12, 1945.

6. "Fish Bowl Grid Game is Booked at Punta Gorda," *The Tampa Tribune,* December 28, 1945.

7. "Even Box Cars Can be a Home," *The Tampa Tribune,* March 24, 1946.

8. "21 Persons Fined in Mayor's Court, *Ft. Myers New-Press,* April 14, 1946.

9. Wikipedia website; "Tampa College," http://en.wikipedia.org/wiki/Tampa_College, accessed May 27, 2015.

10. Vernon Peeples, *Punta Gorda and the Charlotte Harbor Area,* Norfolk/Virginia Beach: The Donning Company, 1986, 144.

11. Wikipedia website; "1947 Fort Lauderdale Hurricane," en.wikipedia.org/wiki/1947_Fort_Lauderdale_hurricane, accessed May 27, 2015.

12. Milton Plumb, "Heifer Sells for $3100 at Ocala Brahman Cattle Show," *The Tampa Tribune,* January 10, 1948.

13. "Charlotte Gets $11,000 Program for Soil Saving," *The Tampa Tribune,"* June 27, 1948.

14. "Sarasota Ships 114 Calves to Texas Rodeos," *The Tampa Tribune,"* August 14, 1948.

15. Milton Plumb, "Million-Dollar Success Story - Working Couple Builds 200,000-Acre Ranch," *The Tampa Sunday Tribune,* August 29, 1948.

16. "Scottish Rite Club Host at Banquet," *Ft. Myers News-Press,* December 26, 1948.

17. "Five Youths Admit Murdock Robbery," *Ft. Myers News Press*, February 22, 1949.

18. "Charlotte Adopts New Tax Roll," *The Tampa Tribune*, July 16, 1949.

19. *Ft. Myers News-Press*, July 17, 1949.

20. "Punta Gorda City Commission Sells Property to Winter Garden Nursery," *Ft. Myers News-Press*, August 4, 1949.

21. "Scottish Right Has Punta Gorda Party," *Ft. Myers News-Press*, August 19, 1949.

22. "Large Alva Ranch Sold for $32,500," *Ft. Myers News-Press*, September 8, 1949.

23. *Ft. Myers News-Press*, September 16, 1949.

24. S. L. Ditto, "Cattlemen Agree to Hunting Permits," *Ft. Myers News-Press*, November 21, 1949.

25. "Charlotte Hotel Scene of Ball," *Ft. Myers News-Press*, January 6, 1950.

26. "Frizzells are Hosts to Scottish Rite," *Ft. Myers News-Press*, February 10, 1950.

27. "OES Initiates 4 New Members," *Ft. Myers News- Press*, March 26, 1950.

28. "$25,000 Sought from Rancher in Car Crash," *The Tampa Tribune*, March 14, 1950.

29. *Ft. Myers New-Press*, April 30, 1950.

30. "$18,000 Damages Sought in Suit," *Ft. Myers News-Press*, May 16, 1950.

31. "Punta Gorda Man Sued for $25,000," *Ft. Myers News-Press*, July 1, 1950.

32. "Plant City Man Wins $3,500 Verdict in Charlotte Suit," *Ft. Myers News-Press*, March 30, 1951.

33. "Frank Smoak Jr. Named Chairman at Party Meeting," *Ft. Myers News-Press*, August 13, 1950.

34. *Ft. Myers News-Press*, September 19, 1950, and January 4, 1951.

35. "Arcadia Broker Asks $25,000 in Charlotte Suit," *The Tampa Tribune*, December 7, 1950.

36. "Big Alva Ranch Brings $136,000," *Ft. Myers New-Press*, December 23, 1950.

37. "Judgment for Rancher Filed in Charlotte," *The Tampa Tribune*, August 7, 1951.

38. "Scottish Rite Club Has Annual Supper and Yule Party," *Ft. Myers News-Press*, December 22, 1950.

39. "31 Cattle Gross $2885 at Charlotte Fair Stock Sale," *The Tampa Tribune*, January 20, 1951.

40. "Frizzell Arrested," *Ft. Myers News-Press*, February 16, 1951.

41. "Charlotte Cattlemen Hosts at Fish Fry," (Ft. Myers News Press, April 5, 1951)

42. "Wildlife Officer Guilty of Selling Quail Resigns Job," *The Tampa Tribune*, May 5, 1951.

43. "Negroes, Permitted to Dig for Money, Leave in a Hurry," *Ft. Myers-News Press*, September 24, 1951.

44. "Cattlemen Attend State Convention," *Ft. Myers News-Press*, November 16, 1951.

45. "Vanderbilts Waste No Time Developing Charlotte Ranch," *The Tampa Tribune*, December 16, 1951.

46. *The Orlando Sentinel*, January 2, 1953.

47. "Charlotte Fair Prizes Awarded," *Ft. Myers News-Press*, January 20, 1952.

48. Don Vincent, "Cattle Clatter," *The Orlando Sentinel*, February 8, 1952.

49. *Ft. Myers News-Press*, March 2, 1952.

50. "Charlotte Ranches Up Fertilizer Use," *Ft. Myers News-Press,* June 25, 1952.

51. "Charlotte Ranchers, Farmers to Control Surface Irrigation," *Ft. Myers News Press,* April 23, 1952.

52. "Cattlemen Plan Tour, Supper at Tuesday Meeting," *Ft. Myers News-Press,* September 7, 1952.

53. "Punta Gorda Home Brings $8,700 at Public Auction," *Ft. Myers News-Press,* September 24, 1952.

54. *Ft. Myers News-Press,* October 29.

55. *Ft. Myers News-Press,* October 30, 1952.

56. *The Tampa Tribune,* January 4, 1953.

57. "Wauchula Man Knows Pheasants Can Live in Florida Wilds," *The Tampa Tribune,* February 1, 1953.

58. "Lumber Yard Sold," *Ft. Myers News-Press,* March 6, 1953.

59. "28 Brahman Cattle Sold at Bartow Bring $18,220 Total," *The Tampa Tribune,* March 22, 1953.

60. "Desoto Board Buys Needed Road Supplies," *The Tampa Tribune,* May 7, 1953.

61. "Card of Thanks," *Ft. Myers News-Press,* May 31, 1953.

62. "McCarty is Expected to Name Entirely New Livestock Board," *The Tampa Tribune,* June 2, 1953.

63. *Ft. Myers News-Press,* July 19, 1953.

64. "U. S. Price Supports for Beef is Aim of New Group Organized at Meet by Some 30 Ranchers, *The Tampa Tribune,* July 28, 1953.

65. "Florida Cattlemen to Ask Benson What Happens to his Mail," *The Tampa Tribune,* October 25, 1953.

66. "Florida Cattlemen Urge Aid for their Industry," *The Tampa Tribune,* October 27, 1953.

67. "Four Generals Spend Thanksgiving Holiday Near Englewood," *The Tampa Tribune,* November 28, 1953.

End of an Era

1. "Chamber Told 32 Homes Being Built in South Venice," *The Tampa Tribune,* January 21, 1954.

2. "Charlotte County Fair Closing Tonight," *Ft. Myers News Press,* January 23, 1954.
3. *The Tampa Tribune,* March 5, 1954.

4. "Tax Credit Given for Used Truck in Punta Gorda," *Ft. Myers News Press,* June 3, 1954.

5. Sam Mase, "A.C. Frizzell - Murdock Man Went From $68 to $2,300,000," *The Tampa Tribune,* July, 1954.

6. Ibid.

7. "Safecrackers Get $3,000 at Murdock Store, Postoffice," *The Tampa Tribune,* December 2, 1955.

8. "Cowboy Gives Up in Fatal Shooting at Punta Gorda," *Ft. Myers News Press,* March 6, 1956.

9. "Englewood Man Held in Killing During Cat Hunt," *The Tampa Tribune,* June 28, 1954.

10. "Carey-Frizzell Vows Exchanged in Murdock Rites," *Ft. Myers News Press,* April 22, 1956.

11. "Charlotte County Will Vote on Fire Control Proposal," *Ft. Myers News Press,* November 4, 1956.

12. "Cattleman Charged with Careless Pasture Burning," *The Tampa Tribune, Tampa Bay Times,* and *Ft. Myers News Press,* November 30, 1956.

13. "Shipping of Watermelons from W. Coast Due Soon," *The Tampa Tribune*, February 3, 1957.

14. "Dump Truck Bumps Charlotte School Bus, No One Hurt," *Ft. Myers News Press*, May 17, 1957.

15. "Roy S. Frizzell Buys Auto Firm," *Ft. Myers News Press*, June 16, 1957.

16. *Ft. Myers News Press*, April 4, 1958.

17. "Lee, Charlotte Businessman Dies," *Ft. Myers News Press*, August 30, 1958.

18. "Zoom! Up, Up, Up Go Punta Gorda Permits," *Tampa Bay Times*, November 16, 1958.

19. "Port Charlotte Rises Rapidly in Area of Former Wilderness," *Ft. Myers News Press*, February 18, 1959.

20. "Woman Held After Girl Dunked in Swim Pool," *Tampa Bay Times*, June 1, 1959.

21. *Between the Bars*, Jennifer Tresh, Author House, September 22, 2010.

22. "Frizzell Lumber Company Will Stage Grand Opening Today," *Ft. Myers News Press*, June 15, 1960.

23. "Fire at Murdock, The Tampa Tribune, December 20, 1960."

BIBLIOGRAPHY

Note: The author has been collecting materials about her family, the Frizzells, for most of her life. The collection includes personal letters, photographs, documents, newspaper articles, books, interviews, memorabilia, and family lore.

Ancestry at www.ancestry.com. City and Area Directories. Various places, various years.

Ancestry at www.ancestry.com. United States Federal Census Collection. Various places, various years.

Atlanta Constitution. January 19, 1920. Classified Ad.

Bergstrom, Micheāl. "Black Pioneer In Charlotte County Fought For What Was His." *Sarasota Herald-Tribune*, July 8, 1993. https://news.google.com/newspapers?nid=1755&dat=19930708&id=MX8fAAAAIBAJ&sjid=vXsEAAAAIBAJ&pg=6625,2309416&hl=en (accessed May 23, 2015).

Bergstrom, Micheāl. "In 30s, Times Were Tough, Especially For Blacks." *Sarasota Herald-Tribune*. August 4, 1994. https://news.google.com/newspapers?nid=1755&dat=19940804&id=z24fAAAAIBAJ&sjid=YHwEAAAAIBAJ&pg=6672,3544174&hl=en (accessed May 19, 2015).

Charlotte County, Florida, History Collections Online. http://ccflhistory.contentdm.oclc.org/cdm/. Various photographs of early Murdock and excerpts from the Daniel Child diaries, gift of Vernon and Edna Jane Peeples.

Charlotte County Historical Center 2012. "McCall Section House" on Cape Haze Pioneer Trail Brochure. http://www.charlottecountyfl.com/CommunityServices/CapeHazeTrailBrochure.pdf (accessed May 5, 2015).

Clendinen, Barbara. "Ways for Using Eggs as Main Dishes Help in Meat Shortage." *The Tampa Tribune*. Apri1 12, 1945.

Custermen website. "WW2 History of the 34th 'Red Bull' Infantry Division - Training for Europe." http://custermen.com/ItalyWW2/Units/Division34.htm (accessed February 15, 2016).

Ditto, S. L.. "Cattlemen Agree to Hunting Permits." *Ft. Myers News-Press.* November 21, 1949.

Farris, Fred. *Once Upon A Time In Southwest Florida.* Venice, Florida: Gondolier Publishing Company, 1982.

Florida Department of Environmental Protection Website. *Cattle Dipping Vats in Florida.* http://www.dep.state.fl.us/water/nonpoint/cdv.htm (accessed July 25, 2015).

Florida Memory. State Archives of Florida. http://floridamemory.com (accessed May 20, 2015). Various photographs.

[1]Florida Railroad Company website. "Florida Logging Railroads." http://www.flarr.com/lumbercos.htm (accessed May 17, 2015).

Forest and Stream Magazine. March 1894.

Ft. Myers News-Press. Some material contained in this book is from the author's collection of articles. Many scattered issues and classified ads are in the collection.

Larkin, Angie. "Old Punta Gorda." *Charlotte Sun.* May 19, 1984.

Martin, Karen. "Teacher, Students Remember School." *Sarasota Herald-Tribune.* February 16, 1989. https://news.google.com/newspapers?nid=1755&dat=19890216&id=eT8gAAAAIBAJ&sjid=XXoEAAAAIBAJ&pg=6350,478809&hl=en (accessed May 22, 2015).

Mase, Sam. "A.C. Frizzell - Murdock Man Went From $68 to $2,300,000." *The Tampa Tribune,* July, 1954.

The Orlando Sentinel. Some material contained in this book is from the author's collection of articles. Several scattered issues are in the collection.

The Orlando Sentinel. Obituaries. "Martha Pearle Vogt." December 14, 2011. http://www.legacy.com/obituaries/orlandosentinel/obituary.aspx?n=martha-pearle-vogt&pid=155035386 (accessed May 26, 2015).

Peeples, Vernon. *Punta Gorda and the Charlotte Harbor Area.* Norfolk, Virginia: The Donning Company, 1986.

Plumb, Milton. "Heifer Sells for $3100 at Ocala Brahman Cattle Show." *The Tampa Tribune.* January 10, 1948.

Plumb, Milton. "Million-Dollar Success Story Working Couple Builds 200,000-Acre Ranch." *The Tampa Sunday Tribune.* August 29, 1948.

Punta Gorda Herald. Some material contained in this book is from the author's collection of articles. Many scattered issues and classified ads are in the collection.

Remington, Frederic. "*Cracker Cowboy*" and "*Arizona Cow-boy.*"

Tampa-Hillsborough County Public Library System. The Burgett Brothers. http://digitalcollections.hcplc.org/digital/collection/p15391coll1/id/2588/rec/1 9 (accessed April 26, 2018). Two photographs.

Tampa Times. Some material contained in this book is from the author's collection of articles.

The Tampa Tribune. Some material contained in this book is from the author's collection of articles. Many scattered issues and classified ads are in the collection, including classified ads that are not otherwise cited in the text of this book.

Trantow, "Russ Lumber Token/Maverick?" http://www.treasurenet.com/forums/tokens-tags/20521-russ-lumber-token-maverick.html (accessed May 23, 2015).

Tresh, Jennifer. *Between the Bars.* Author House, September 22, 2010.

Vincent, Don. "Cattle Clatter." *The Orlando Sentinel.* February 8, 1952.

Where to Stop A Guide to the Best Hotels in the World. Published by Moses King, Boston, Massachusetts, 1894-1895.

Wikipedia. "Cowboy."
http://en.wikipedia.org/wiki/Cowboy (accessed May 22, 2015).

Wikipedia. "1947 Fort Lauderdale Hurricane. "
en.wikipedia.org/wiki/1947_Fort_Lauderdale_hurricane (accessed May 27, 2015).

Wikipedia. "Tampa College."
http://en.wikipedia.org/wiki/Tampa_College (accessed May 27, 2015).

Williams, Lindsey. "Byron Rhode Recalls His Early Years In Punta Gorda." September 5, 1993. http://www.lindseywilliams.org/index.htm?Articles/Byron_Rhode_Recalls_His_Early_Years_In_Punta_Gorda.htm~mainFrame (accessed October 3, 2018).

Williams, Lindsey. "CIA Held Secret Training in Webb Wildlife Area." July 31, 1994. http://www.lindseywilliams.org/index.htm?Articles/CIA_Held_Secret_Training_In_Webb_Wildlife_Area.htm~mainFrame (accessed May 20, 2015).